The Penny
Poet of
Portsmouth

The Penny Poet of Portsmouth

A Memoir of Place, Solitude, and Friendship

Katherine Towler

COUNTERPOINT

Berkeley

Library of Congress Cataloging-in-Publication Data Is Available

Cover design by Kelly Winton
Interior design by Tabitha Lahr

ISBN 978-1-61902-712-1

Counterpoint Press
2560 Ninth Street, Suite 318
Berkeley, CA 94710
www.counterpointpress.com

Printed in the United States of America
Distributed by Publishers Group West

10 9 8 7 6 5 4 3 2 1

Author's Note:
I have recreated events and conversations from my memories of them,
journal entries and notes made at the time, and the help of others. While
all the stories in this book are true, some names have been changed to
protect the privacy of the people involved.

In memory of Robert Dunn and in gratitude for the community of writers he treasured in New Hampshire.

How is it they insist
that you must have a known address
who nowhere have a home?

—*Robert Dunn*

The Penny Poet of Portsmouth

Preface

Around town, it was said that he lived on air, though he really lived on coffee and cigarettes. He was a union of unlikely opposites—one of the strangest and loveliest of people, one of the poorest and richest, one of the most sardonic and serious. He could be brilliant and intentionally obtuse, or quietly contained and defiant, all in the same moment. At first I was simply his neighbor, and we knew each other by proximity. Over time we came to recognize each other as fellow writers, secret rebels trying to get something down that speaks to others. Later I became a friend, in the fashion that he had friends. We traded conversation and the titles of books as we drank tea or wine. He let me in, but only a little, and only because he had no choice. In the end, I was someone indefinable to either of us, part family, part nurse, part surprised bystander. How I came to be that person and what it taught me is this story, though it is one that remains riddled with certain mysteries, just as his life remains a book of blank pages on which he left only the poems.

I.

Port City

1.

Whidden Street

~~~

Barely a block long, Whidden Street comes to a dead end at the edge of South Mill Pond and has no real business being called a street. Houses pressed close together face each other across a strip of pavement not much wider than a hallway, their shuttered facades suggesting a scene from an antique postcard. In their mix of colors, cranberry red and white and mustard yellow, the older houses have the solid look of something that has been here a long time. Others are of a more recent vintage, rougher upstarts that match the broken pavement on their front stoops.

Our first night in our new house on Whidden Street, I stood at the window and gazed out at the rooftops bathed in the glow from the single streetlight. I had lived in other New England cities, but none of them had felt this old or this quirky, the very shape of the streets telling the story of the past. It was midnight, and I still hadn't found the sheets in the maze of boxes that surrounded me. The sound of bells tolling the hour made me pause for a moment in my frenzy of unpacking. Though the steeple was blocks away in Market Square, it seemed I could reach out the window and touch those solemn notes. They brought the night close and made the darkness familiar in an unfamiliar place.

The dank smell of the pond came in through the window, mud laced with a hint of fish, and in the other direction from downtown I heard the piercing note of a boat's whistle out on the river. The hourly tolling of the bells and the traffic on the river would become the soundtrack of my new life, noises that would soon fade into the background, but on that hot night in June of 1991, when I finally arrived somewhere I would stay longer than six months or a year, they struck me as the essence of this place I could not quite believe I was going to call home.

For more than a decade, since graduating from college, I had wandered up and down the Eastern seaboard in a restless search for a job, a relationship, and a life that made sense. All too often, I had packed everything I owned into a hatchback and started over, certain that another beginning would be the answer. This time I wasn't making the move alone, and I was taking up residence in an actual house, not a one-room studio apartment. The man I was about to marry had driven a U-Haul truck loaded with both our possessions from Boston that morning and now searched through the mess of boxes with me, as exhausted and apprehensive as I was, both of us nervous and excited to discover where we had landed. In retrospect, our arrival in New Hampshire has a sense of inevitability, the moment when I finally stopped running, but that night as I sorted through our ill-packed possessions, I felt like I was standing in a doorway waiting to see whether I would step through to the other side.

We were woken at five-thirty the next morning by a very loud and raspy voice barking out the declaration, "Gonna be a hot one." When I raised myself on one elbow and drew back the curtain, I saw a large, unshaven man standing beneath the window in the middle of the street. He wore paint-splattered work pants and construction boots. Beside him stood a petite woman in her sixties with a stack of newspapers in her arms. She handed him one and said, "If it burns off."

"Oh, it'll burn off all right," he said.

The woman went back up the street, but he remained beneath our window with a coffee mug in one hand and the newspaper in the other, glancing from side to side as though expecting someone else to appear and continue the conversation. I would learn that Ed greeted the woman who delivered the newspaper like this every morning.

Fog hung over the pond in a milky sheen that gave the water the look of a clouded mirror. I made my way down the back stairs to the kitchen, thinking that even the weather here had an old-fashioned feel, the wispy fog seeming to trace the shape of tall ships coming into the harbor. The steps beneath my feet were worn down, hollowed into small depressions by nearly two centuries of use, and they were so narrow I had to descend carefully to avoid tumbling straight down the whole flight.

The existence of this staircase was one of the house's idiosyncrasies. It was only a few feet from the front staircase, which rose from the hallway right inside the front door. Why two sets of stairs were necessary in such a small house was a mystery. This had never been a grand residence, even in the 1800s, the sort of place that might require a second staircase for the maid. I would become used to making the mental calculation—front stairs or back?—several times a day, a choice that seemed to link me to a host of people who had gone before me in this place.

I walked through the rooms strewn with random pieces of furniture, rolled-up rugs, and stray lamps, uncertain where to begin. It was then that I heard someone sneeze. Jim, I thought, still upstairs, but a moment later I heard him opening the refrigerator and realized the sneeze had come from a different direction. I crept to the window in the bathroom and peered around the edge of the frame. The profile of a woman was clearly visible behind a curtained window level with mine and only a yard away. She was setting a coffee mug on a table. It appeared that we were going to get to know our neighbors well.

The house needed a good cleaning before we could even begin to unpack, and after breakfast I unearthed the vacuum and set to work. The place had clearly seen hard use by previous tenants; the walls were pockmarked with nail holes, and the paint was worn. Still, it felt like a palace to me, with three rooms downstairs and three upstairs. I wasn't used to having this much space, and I found the sloped floors and narrow closets with their tiny, latched doors fascinating. Evidence of just how old this house was—1830, the rental agent had told us—was there wherever I turned: the thin lintels of the mantelpieces, the ceramic doorknobs with their amber hue, the antique glass in the windows that gave the scene on the other side a wavering quality, like a drawing done in sand. I was enthralled with this shabby old place, with the idea of living in a house so quintessentially New England.

When I set off later that morning to find a supermarket, I stepped out the front door directly onto the street. There was no room for a sidewalk. Cars did not belong here, though the residents owned them, of course, in some cases two or three vehicles to a house. Where to put all these cars, we would discover, was a constant source of conflict. I had to inch out of the single spot beside our house to avoid hitting the house across the street.

When I returned from the supermarket, a towheaded boy came running from a house a few down from ours, extended his hand, and said, "Welcome to Whidden Street." He went on to recite a litany of facts about dinosaurs at a rapid speed that made it impossible to follow half of what he said. At the end of this breathless outburst, he said, "I'm Nate. I'm six. Do you have a cat?"

Yes, I told him, we did have a cat.

"I thought I saw a new cat."

"Was he gray?" I asked.

"Yup, gray."

"That's Zane."

Nate nodded and zipped off as quickly as he had come.

We met most of our neighbors over the next few days. It was hard to avoid, living in such close quarters. Eleanor came over to introduce herself from the house directly across the street, where she lived with her mother and her niece. Her parents had owned the place since the 1940s, she told us, and she had grown up there. Eleanor belonged to the group of old-timers on the block whose houses, like ours, remained pretty close to their original states. Nate's family was in the other camp, recent transplants who had restored their antique houses to a polished authenticity. Being renters, we fell somewhere in between the two groups. No matter how long any of us had been there or where we had come from, though, we were united by the cats. Whidden Street really belonged to them.

We had just Zane, a fiercely smart and independent stray Jim had taken in down in Boston, where he had been living when we met, but our neighbors had two or three each, which meant that the felines outnumbered the humans on the block. The lone plot of grass adjoined our house, and it was here that the cats congregated and engaged in a contest to determine who would rule this corner of town. The contest had been decided before we arrived on the scene—Roscoe, a mean orange tabby, would tear up any cat who challenged him—but Roscoe felt compelled to remind the other cats of this fact on a regular basis.

Those first weeks in Portsmouth, I went out walking, exploring the town by wandering its maze of skinny streets. Most days I encountered a tiny, gaunt man somewhere on my route—crossing

Market Square, emerging from the post office, or seated on the stone wall by the eighteenth-century gravestones on Pleasant Street. He moved with a slow deliberation, shoulders hunched forward, in a flimsy black trench coat and a flat cap, a styrofoam coffee cup in one hand and a cigarette between the fingers of the other. His face was framed by glasses with thick, black rims, and a bristled mustache obscured his lips. He might have been in his late forties or early seventies; there was no way to tell. He seemed to be a fixture downtown, a part of the streetscape, and I assumed from this and his worn clothes that he was homeless. He had the look of someone who wandered with no destination and might not have eaten in some time.

This strange, little man moving like a leaf nudged by the wind, his body bent in such a stoop that he appeared not much more than five feet in height, though he was clearly taller, belonged among these streets that had once been cow paths. He struck me as a figure, like so much in the landscape of Portsmouth, out of another century. One afternoon when I happened to glance out the window at the right moment, I saw him passing by our house. What was he doing, I wondered, all the way at the dead end of Whidden Street? The next day I paid closer attention and caught him emerging from the house on the other side of our patch of lawn, by the pond. Shortly after this, I stepped onto the street one day just as he did so. He raised his head, and his eyes darted away, the only acknowledgment I received.

Our house, like many in the neighborhood, had a dirt cellar. When I took the shallow stairs into its dank depths, I could see the rock ledge on which the foundation rested, jutting from the dirt wall behind the furnace. Almost two centuries earlier, the earth had been carved to hold the house, and it was easy to imagine men with shovels executing the job. A window not much bigger than a business envelope was cut into the base of the foundation. We left the window unlatched so Zane could go in and out. When the garbage men backed their truck down Whidden Street, he would fly through the window and race upstairs to hide under the couch.

One evening we found Zane crouched by the basement door hissing. Further investigation revealed Roscoe pressed to a moldy corner of the basement. We propped the window open, but he did not budge. After fifteen minutes of attempting to coax him toward the window, we went out into the yard to call him from the other side.

Jim and I were standing next to the house, calling Roscoe's name, when the diminutive man I had observed downtown came down the street. It was a cool night, and he was wearing a brown corduroy jacket that looked like a relic from the 1960s instead of his trench coat. He stopped when he reached us and said, "We have a renegade cat, do we?"

I had not articulated it to myself, but clearly I had formed an expectation of what it might be like to hear him talk, because I was so startled by his speech. I explained that Roscoe was in the basement, refusing to come out.

He bent down by the basement window and called, "Roscovitch, my dear Roscovitch, do come here."

He sounded like he was reciting Shakespeare in his soft and lilting voice. After a moment, Roscoe jumped through the window and went darting toward the house next door.

"I do apologize," he said. "But I'm afraid that cat has a mind of his own."

I thanked him, but he had already turned away and evaporated down the bit of pavement between our houses.

2.

Here and There

⌒

B efore I met Jim, writing was my life, the reason for getting up in the morning and going to bed at night, the justification for any number of choices that sometimes baffled my friends and family. Quitting jobs repeatedly, for instance, and once again packing up my boxes of books and moving on. In my nomadic existence, I was like a junkie looking for the next fix. If only I had a different job, or no job at all, or lived with roommates to reduce the rent, or lived alone so I could have more privacy, then I would truly be able to write, and I would finish at least one of the novels I had started. These were the sorts of arguments I carried on with myself as I bet on one compromise versus another and cursed the need to make a living. Artists' colonies offered temporary refuge, where I could live for a few months at a time on the largesse of the donors who supported them, but once the divinely empty days at the artists' colonies came to an end, I had to go somewhere and make money again. At a time when many of my female friends were getting married and having babies, I was obsessed with something else entirely, an intense desire for months of uncharted time and hours of unbroken silence.

I began writing poems when I was ten years old in a marble bound notebook. They were terrifically bad, sentimental poems, but my teachers encouraged me, especially Mrs. Melchior in sixth grade, who suggested maybe I would become a writer. I don't know that it was her quiet suggestion that set a direction for me, because in many ways I had been a writer from the time I started reading and became smitten with books and making up stories in my head, but by high school, the idea had a sure hold on me. In the New York City apartment where I grew up, I often stayed in my bedroom with the door closed, seated at a huge desk we had acquired from a neighbor who no longer wanted it. If I wasn't writing in my journal or composing a poem or a story, I was reading. I went to parties and smoked pot with my best friend, and had a boyfriend briefly in eleventh grade. In the summer, my family spent August at the beach in Rhode Island, where I lay for hours in the sun with the other teenagers listening to our transistor radios. But behind and beneath all this, my other life ran like a stream. The life of words was where I spent my real time.

As I grew older, it gradually dawned on me that not everyone led a double life. I didn't want to have children. I wasn't particularly interested in getting married, even. Mostly I was focused on protecting the secret life of the writing. American culture does not encourage this sort of thing. We're a society of extroverts and overachievers bowing to the gods of money and extreme measures of success. The slow growth of the writer, much of it occurring out of sight, in solitude, does not register. I had no guides for my secret life, no training. My parents and teachers did not tell me how to cultivate an ability to spend hours alone. I had to learn this on my own.

* * *

The desire for those hours alone had not left me, but I needed to make room for more now. I set up my office in a bedroom on the second floor of our house on Whidden Street and settled into a routine of writing in the morning and turning to my paid freelance work in the afternoon. I was writing what a fellow writer referred to as my "third first novel" (two others sat in a box in the closet, unfinished). When Jim and I met, a year and a half before we moved to Portsmouth, I told him I was halfway through a draft of the book. He liked to tease me about the fact that I was still halfway through the draft, which would, in fact, remain the case for several more years. I am not a fast writer, and it became apparent after our arrival in Portsmouth that where I had been living and how, with roommates or without them, were not the determining factors I had imagined them to be in whether I could complete the manuscript. Writing a novel required bucket loads of persistence and confidence, which I was able to muster only fleetingly.

A couple of days after our encounter with the man next door over Roscoe's refusal to leave the basement, I went out to water the marigolds we had planted in a bit of dirt about a foot wide in front of the house. Eleanor came down her front steps with a big pocketbook like the one my grandmother used to carry tucked beneath her arm. We traded greetings and then she said, "I saw you had some trouble with Roscoe the other night." Nothing went unnoticed on Whidden Street. "Robert has a way with him. He won't come for anyone else."

"Our cat was a little agitated at having him in the basement."

She made a clucking noise. "I can imagine." She leaned forward and said in a low voice, glancing quickly from side to side to make sure we were not overheard, "That Roscoe is a bully."

I nodded in agreement and watched her climb into her oversized car and carefully maneuver it down the block, backing up the whole way.

Now I knew his name—Robert. In its simplicity and formality, it seemed to suit him. From other neighbors I discovered that, like us, Robert was a renter who occupied a single room on the second floor of the house by the pond. His landlady, Connie Wilson, had lived on Whidden Street most of her life. A short, plump woman in her late seventies, Connie stepped onto the street in the morning in a flowered housecoat to call the cats in a tone that managed to be tough and sweet at the same time. She had a weakness for stray cats, who, in the way of stray cats everywhere, seemed to know that hers was the door to knock on. There were three of them under her roof when we arrived, including the notorious Roscoe, and a little dachshund she carried in her arms like a baby.

Robert's room was on the far side of the house, so I could not see him behind a filmy curtain when I sat at my desk writing in the morning. I could keep an eye on the cats, though, and frequently left off mid-sentence to dash downstairs and break up a fight. From my desk, I had a view of the pond, where an occasional mallard went paddling by, and in our yard there was a rickety shed festooned with faded lobster buoys hanging from it like Christmas ornaments. Not much happened in the frame of this view, other than the cat fights. I could get lost in the imagined world of the writing with nothing to call me back.

In the afternoons when I was done with my freelance work, I often walked into town to the post office or bank. If I passed Robert on my way across Market Square, he would slide by me without looking up, though I was usually certain he had seen me and must have recognized me. His lowered head did not invite interruption.

Finished with my errands, I would stop in at J.J. Newberry's, the five-and-dime on Congress Street. The cavernous space of the store was filled with a warren of aisles containing shampoo and thread, school supplies and cheap dishware, Halloween costumes and little plastic pails to take to the beach. In the pet section in the back, parakeets chirped in their cages and goldfish swam in circles. The soda fountain ran along a wall toward the front, near the plate glass window looking out on the square. A collection of older men and women spent a good part of the day there drinking coffee, seated on stools covered in red vinyl. Many of these regulars lived in one of the public housing apartment buildings a few blocks away, cinderblock structures distinguished by a complete absence of any architectural design and the folks out front smoking cigarettes.

Like those who spent the day at J.J. Newberry's, I could be flexible with my time, at least when I was not on deadline with a project for a client. I recognized myself in the aimlessness of the teenagers playing Hacky Sack in front of the North Church and the retired men and women lined up on the stools at the soda fountain. They were taking in the scene, as I was, for the simple sake of doing so. I liked to stroll through Newberry's just to be reminded of how much really doesn't matter.

I expected to find Robert at Newberry's when I stopped in to examine the plastic change purses and the little rain bonnets in their sealed packets, but I never did. Too much talking went on at Newberry's, I would realize when I came to know him better. He preferred to observe downtown life from a distance, which was, in many ways, my approach as well. I exchanged brief remarks about the weather with the women behind the cash registers who wore patterned smocks and had rows of tight, permed curls hugging their heads. I eavesdropped on the conversations at the soda fountain without partaking of the hot dogs or oil-slicked coffee. The old men with their jackets hunched around their shoulders looked like figures in a Kodachrome. Everything in Newberry's had that slightly yellowed tinge around the edges. I lost myself in the flattened-out, 1950s feel of the place before making my way home for another session of writing.

* * *

I was seated at my desk working one afternoon when I was interrupted by a knock on the front door. I went downstairs to find Eleanor waiting with a large ceramic bowl in her hands. She beamed at me and said, "It's starter for a friendship cake." I peered through the piece of plastic wrap stretched over the bowl. The murky liquid, vaguely pink in color, had a gelatin-like consistency. Eleanor handed me a typed sheet of instructions along with the bowl. For thirty days, various things were to be added to the starter (two and a half cups of sugar, canned peaches, maraschino cherries), and the contents of the bowl stirred twice a day. It should not be refrigerated. At two weeks, the starter would begin to foam. This was normal. After thirty days, I was to drain off some liquid to pass on for the next batch and add packaged cake and pudding mix to the remainder before baking it into a cake.

I left the bowl on the kitchen counter until Jim came home. Together we cautiously lifted the plastic wrap and sniffed this stuff that was both fascinating and disgusting. We dutifully added the required ingredients over the coming weeks, though I drew the line at the cherries as too unnatural. As we watched the pink gunk grow, it became clear to both of us that we had no intention of turning this into something we would eat. Once the thirty days had passed, we tossed the frothy mess in the trash and returned the empty bowl to Eleanor.

The friendship cake incident, as we came to think of it, was emblematic of life in Portsmouth, where the unannounced arrival of someone at the door was not unusual. This took getting used to. Having grown up in Manhattan, I was still to some extent a city girl accustomed to the anonymity of being one among many, invisible in the crowd. We had not been in Portsmouth long before I knew enough people that a walk into town inevitably meant stopping to talk with someone. I could not leave my house unnoticed, and at first I found this disorienting.

I had never considered living in New Hampshire. Vermont, with its rolling hills and alternative politics, was where I saw myself. Its darker and more conservative twin, New Hampshire, was not my kind of place, or so I had assumed, though I wasn't really looking for a home. When we met, Jim introduced me to the concept of the geographic cure and suggested ever so gently that perhaps the idea that moving would solve my problems had motivated my travels up and down the East Coast. This was the sort of observation that, as a psychologist, he was qualified to make. I readily recognized the truth in it.

Jim's job brought us to Portsmouth. He saw an ad for a private practice that was looking to add a psychologist and answered it. We had stopped once in Portsmouth for lunch, but that was the extent of our knowledge of the town. The move was not made on a whim, as many of mine had been, but it still had the feel of chance.

In the years when I moved twenty times, give or take a few, I had a vaguely articulated notion that staying in one place too long would make me stale. To gather material for my writing I needed to observe people and places with the eye of the newcomer and the outsider. Wasn't the genius of Ernest Hemingway or James Joyce or Gertrude Stein linked to their being exiles, people whose homes, if they had them, were temporary or adopted?

I fell into a pattern throughout these years of retreating from the world only to rush back to it. I could not sustain the isolation I craved and ricocheted between bouts of intensive social experiences and periods of solitude. This pattern worked in a mad way, though frequently I lost control of it, things like work and family and Christmas having a tendency to intrude. When I could not find time alone,

I became edgy and depressed, unmoored from what truly seemed to matter—that inner journey, that exploration of empty corridors, that road into the self. Writing was the reason for this journey, but there were times when it felt more like the excuse.

I wanted people in my life and didn't want them at the same time. In the end, though, I wanted the writing most of all, and this won out over a sustained, close relationship or any notion of a career. It took all my resources to shut out the din of ordinary human life and go after this elusive thing.

To devote myself to writing with the single-minded attention it required did not leave room for a spouse; I could do one or the other, but not both. In my late twenties and early thirties, I was ruled by this sort of either/or thinking as I shot like a pinball from one place to another and one emotional stance to another. Now I was going to step beyond the dichotomies I had defined for myself and trade my carefully guarded pools of solitude, at times so vital, at others so lonely, for a shared life. Jim and I were both turning thirty-five in a couple of months, old enough that we had begun to consider skipping marriage altogether, but to our mutual surprise and nervous delight, we were planning a wedding for September.

Deciding to get married felt weighty enough, but in some ways becoming a known person in a known place struck me as even weightier. I was not going to make a glancing blow at Portsmouth and move on, as I had done so often before. I was in the process of becoming a member of a community that would refuse to ignore me even if I wanted to be ignored. Portsmouth wooed me, though, just as Jim had.

I could take a couple of different routes when I walked into town from Whidden Street—down Pleasant Street past houses dating to the 1700s, one of them once inhabited by an early governor of New Hampshire, or along the river by the historic structures of Strawbery Banke, our living history museum, spelled the way the original British settlers in 1623 spelled Portsmouth's first name. The brick sidewalks in the old Puddle Dock neighborhood, as it was known in past times, are weathered and full of character with their contoured dips and slopes. They are narrow enough that when you meet people coming toward you, you must make room for them to pass. It's customary to say hello. There's an intimacy to these slender walkways and the equally slender streets they border that makes a trip into town feel like a small voyage, a tour through history. There is no news feed dancing before the eyes here, no sense that there might be news to discover. Everything has been discovered already.

The first British settlers came to Portsmouth seeking financial opportunity rather than religious freedom, and the city was a commercial hub for trade in fish and lumber. In the Colonial era, Portsmouth was the fourth largest city in America, a major port on the East Coast, and a center for shipbuilding. The grand houses built by ship captains and merchants are vestiges of this period of prosperity. In the centuries to follow, Portsmouth took on a rougher character. Fortunately, the city's economic decline meant that many of the historic houses and downtown buildings were never torn down.

Many of the antique houses in the South End, the neighborhood where we lived, were constructed in a time when the city's workers did not have the luxury of so much space, with small rooms and low ceilings to conserve heat. The spacious lots that have come to define housing in suburban America have no place here. To walk the streets of Portsmouth is to escape, for a few moments, that America. The Georgian and Federal style buildings are sedate and beautiful, a visual feast. The brick sidewalks gather the sunlight in their warm hues. Yet unlike some other coastal New England cities, the Portsmouth I discovered when we moved here was not a study in preservation but a place with plenty of gritty edges and a strong working-class history.

As I wandered along the river in the late afternoon, the windows of the old houses seemed to nod at me, as if to say that they, too, wanted to escape the modern world, to remember empty days and the pages of long books. There was no need to have a destination, this landscape affirmed, no need to make every thought public. What was new did not feel as necessary—or frankly as new—here. I loved stepping out the front door into another century.

* * *

Connie's house was a two-story New Englander, as they are called in these parts, a big box that sat at the end of Whidden Street on an elevated spot above the pond. Ed was another of the house's inhabitants, one whose voice we grew accustomed to, and not just at five-thirty in the morning. Ed could frequently be heard bellowing up and down the street, sending out strings of curses that got tangled up with the cats' shrieks. He sounded angry much of the time, though once we got to know him, we discovered that his drunken incoherence consisted primarily of blathering at top volume in a bid for attention that seldom appeared to be returned as he went on shouting into the void.

Ed was Connie's nephew, and he worked, when he was employed, as a housepainter. For a while Ed had a job with the city, doing road repair work and other odd jobs out of the Public Works Department. One of the city pickup trucks used to back down Whidden Street at seven in the morning, and Ed would climb into the bed of the truck and ride off, calling out to everyone they passed. There were days when he was too drunk or hungover to work, when he was brought home early or didn't go in at all, and eventually he lost the job.

Ed was a large man with broad shoulders and impressive hands, which made the way he shuffled along that much harder to watch. He wore his old pair of green work pants and a frayed plaid shirt on ninety-degree days and forty-degree days. When it got colder than that, he added a ragged jacket. He would call out my name when he spotted me in the yard or passed me on the street downtown. "Ain't life grand?" he would say, his tone a mixture of resignation and exuberance.

One afternoon I was seated in a lawn chair on the plot of grass by our house when Ed came ambling up the street. He stopped, gazed at the book in my lap, and said, "Reading the hymnal, huh?"

I had been flipping through the book, quietly humming to myself. "We need a couple of hymns for our wedding," I explained.

"What's that, the Episcopal hymnal?"

I nodded yes.

"I thought you were a good Episcopal girl."

I smiled. It was an identity I would never shake, though I had tried.

"What have you got?" he asked.

"'Love Divine, All Loves Excelling.' Or 'Come Down, O Love Divine.'"

"Old standards. You can't go wrong with that."

"You haven't seen my cat, have you?" I said.

"No. When did you see him last?"

"A few hours ago."

"He's probably just sleeping somewhere."

"He doesn't disappear this long usually."

"Christ, it's hot. Can't you let sleeping cats lie?" He barked out this pronouncement and lumbered away.

Once Ed learned I was a writer, he would recite the titles of the books he was currently reading, many of them dense works of history, when he spotted me outside the house. He told me one day that he had just received a letter from Gore Vidal.

"Gore Vidal?" I repeated, certain I had heard him wrong.

"The writer, Gore Vidal. You know him?"

"I know who he is."

"I wrote him a long time ago, after I read one of his books. He's written me a few times. The guy's damned smart."

I never saw any of the letters from Gore Vidal, but Ed convinced me that they existed.

* * *

At first I thought Robert might be another relation of Connie's, though it was hard to imagine Robert and Ed in the same family, even as distant cousins. I learned more after answering a knock on the door one day to find a blonde woman about my age dressed in jeans and a blouse. Clare introduced herself and explained that she lived on the block just behind mine. She turned and pointed at the corner of a house showing beyond a neighbor's yard. A woman I had worked with in New York was an old friend of Clare's, and she suggested that we should meet, though she had no idea that Clare and I lived within sight of each other.

Clare had been in Portsmouth for twenty years and worked as a freelance writer for *The Boston Globe*. Over lunch at a café later that week, she told me Robert's story. He was a poet, quite a good one, in fact. He assembled his poems into little books he sewed together by hand and sold for a penny. For this he had become known as the "Penny Poet of Portsmouth." Clare had written a profile of Robert for the New Hampshire section of the Sunday *Globe* a few years back, an assignment she described as a nightmare. "I proposed the article because I thought he was this interesting character," she said. "I asked him where he had lived before he came to Portsmouth. He said, 'Here and there.' I asked him what he had done for work. He said, 'This and that.' His résumé was one big hole. I realized I was going to have to make an article out of all these holes."

These were the few facts about Robert's life she had been able to glean: He had rented a room in Connie's house for as long as anyone could remember and worked each afternoon at the Athenaeum, a private library in Market Square. He had attended the University of New Hampshire and gone south one summer in the 1960s with the civil rights movement. He was younger than he looked.

* * *

Ed came by one Friday as I was packing the car for a weekend in Vermont. "Where are you headed?" he asked with his usual gruffness.

When I told him, he said, "Bring Connie a newspaper. She loves to read newspapers from other places."

On our return, I went next door. "I've always wanted to go to Vermont," Connie said when I presented her with a copy of *The Caledonian Record*. "I guess I won't get there now." She had been to York, Maine, just over the river once on the trolley, but she had not traveled much farther than that, she said. I thought of the woman in Sarah Orne Jewett's *The Country of the Pointed Firs*, who had never left the small island off the coast of Maine where she was born.

"Won't you come in?" Connie asked.

I was too startled to say no and followed her into a dark hallway. A partially opened door just inside showed a bedroom. She quickly reached for the door handle and pulled it closed. "That's my room," she said. "Ed and Robert are upstairs. We'll go in the kitchen here."

The narrow hall led to another closed door, which she opened to reveal a small kitchen.

"I can make some tea," she said.

"That's all right. I can just stay a minute."

"I'm afraid tea's about all I've got. I'm out of milk at the moment. I guess I need to get to the store."

"I don't need anything. Really," I said.

I took a seat across from Connie at a metal table that looked like it might fall over if either of us breathed too heavily. The kitchen was nearly as dark as the hallway. Sheer curtains at two small squares of window let in a vague light. The walls were covered in peeling patches of wallpaper in some spots, and peeling paint in others, all of it layered in a gray sheen that looked like the residue of some long-ago fire. The refrigerator appeared to be older than I was and made a loud groaning hum. On the other side of another closed door I could hear a television.

To say that Connie's house was run-down, or perhaps the kinder "neglected," does not do it justice. The interior had the feel of a place forgotten by time. The furniture, the appliances, and the splotched walls all seemed to have been untouched since the 1930s. The place would have been shocking were it not so fascinating, a time capsule into which I had stepped. Connie had been sitting at this table in this dim room for most of the century.

"Ed tells me you're a writer," Connie said. "What do you write?"

"I'm working on a novel," I said.

"Is it a mystery?"

"Not exactly."

"I like a mystery. Robert's a writer, you know. I tell people he's like the man who came to dinner. He showed up twenty years ago to rent a room and never left. I didn't really plan on having a boarder that long. He just never left. He's got his work at the Athenaeum. That gets him out a bit. I don't know exactly what he does there, but he seems to like it fairly well. It's good he has that. It gets him out." She repeated this last sentence with a cluck of her tongue, as if implying that I knew what she meant. "I guess he's got his friends in town who are poets. I've never met any of them."

Connie spoke about Robert as though she, like everyone else, had merely observed him walking to and fro and wondered about his strange life. I suppose the fact of his renting a room from her for twenty years was not enough to make him less of an enigma, but as I made my way home, I speculated even more than I had already about the nature of this unusual household and its occupants.

Stepping into Connie's house was like stepping into Faulkner's story "A Rose for Emily," about a woman who has not gone outside in years. Like Miss Emily, Connie was rumored to have received a reprieve on paying property taxes until her death, when the town would take possession of the house, but unlike Miss Emily, she was cheerful and adept at conversation, a part of the world of our neighborhood.

Robert, in his solitary way, was very much a part of our neighborhood, too. I was grateful to have him next door, whether we ever spoke or not.

3.

Moving Closer

J im and I had not lived together before moving to Portsmouth; in fact, both of us had been living alone for a number of years. We told people, only half joking, that we were getting married just in time, before we had become so entrenched in our independent ways it never could have worked. On a breezy Saturday in September, with a thick cover of clouds and a flock of geese overhead as we processed in, we were married at my father's church in Rhode Island. We returned to Portsmouth with a car full of gifts and a changed sense of ourselves. Owning two sets of matched china, one for "every day" and one for special occasions, and cooking pots that had not been purchased at the local Goodwill made me feel that I had grown up overnight. And then there were those vows, with their awe-inspiring permanence. Before standing at the altar and saying those words, the most binding agreements I had made involved signing leases and promising to repay my student loans.

One evening a few weeks after the wedding, Jim came into the bedroom and found me sitting in bed, propped on pillows, staring at the ceiling. "What are you doing?" he asked.

I was in my usual posture for reading, but I wasn't reading. "Thinking," I said.

Thinking, I said, because I didn't want to admit that what I was really doing was writing in my head.

"Thinking about what?" he said.

"Oh, I don't know." I shrugged and added, "My book."

I felt self-conscious being caught in this state, which was my most interior and private, but there was more to my unease than that. I was often writing in my head in the weeks after our wedding, just as I had been in the weeks before, and it seemed, at times, like a betrayal. I wasn't there, in the room with him; I was somewhere else.

I was used to being somewhere else, of course, since I had been doing this for years, but I had not been doing it while living intimately with someone, except for one short period in my early twenties. I had always known that writing was a demanding mistress, though I understood this in more vivid and troubling ways now. I couldn't just shut the door and disappear whenever this mistress called, at any time of the day or night. Someone else needed and wanted and expected me to be present.

Being present. This may be the greatest challenge of marriage for writers and non-writers alike. Being present to another person on a daily basis, or at least attempting it, is a humbling experience that constantly tests our insistence on ego and control. I wasn't particularly good at it, but as time went on, I saw that my failings could not be blamed entirely on the writing. Other people, I noticed, appeared to have just as hard a time at this as I did, whether they were lawyers or grocery store clerks or sculptors.

That fall I began teaching in the Artists-in-the-Schools program in New Hampshire. With this new job, part-time and erratic as it was, and Jim coming home at the end of the day ready for dinner and conversation, I did not have as many unscheduled hours as I did at the artists' colonies or when I lived alone for two winters out in Provincetown at the tip of Cape Cod. The novel went dead on me. This was not the first time this had happened, nor would it be the last, and I knew being married was not the cause. There was just as great a risk, maybe greater, of the writing going flat when I was alone. In an attempt to find my way back into the story, I left my office and walked into town with a loose-leaf folder full of pages in my backpack.

The library smelled of wet wool, and the stairs to the second floor groaned under my weight like massive pines bent in the wind. I threaded around shelves with books spilling out of them, some stacked in piles on the floor, to a small table in the corner. Here I was largely out of sight, but I could keep an eye on the library regulars slumped back in easy chairs reading magazines or sleeping. Some were residents of the local homeless shelter who hung out in Market Square in better weather; others, from the public housing apartments, went back and forth between the library and J.J. Newberry's all day. This gave the place the feel of a drop-in center. I was serenaded by loud snoring while I wrote.

I took comfort in the bowed shelves surrounding me as I scratched lines on paper, crossed them out, and wrote them again. Someday maybe I could add my own book to those shelves. The process of writing a novel, so strange and yet so compelling, went like this, a step forward and a step back, rewriting the same scenes over and over until I made myself believe them. The characters became another family, people I lived with on a daily basis who nonetheless continued to mystify me.

The tall windows on the second floor framed a view of the North Church steeple and the downtown rooftops. I was grateful for that view, even for the snoring men in their hoodies and tattered sweatpants, on the days when I struggled with the writing. This town with its meandering streets and long history held me close. My writing, which floated in an untethered state, airy and out in space somewhere, was brought down to earth here. I was reminded that I had something in common with this odd collection of folks who claimed the library, and Portsmouth, as home. I was situated, along with the words floating across all those pages in front of me, in a time and place that had little use for my literary aspirations.

I went home for lunch but often walked into town later in the afternoon. This was an opportunity to run into Robert, and he was frequently there, marking a stooped path along Congress Street on his way to the post office. If I stepped directly in front of him and said hello when I met him in the post office lobby, he would raise his eyes and return the greeting. I felt that I had committed an act of violation when I did this. On the street, I would see him approaching and ready myself to speak, but when he did not look up, I would let him move past and go on.

Sometimes I stopped to watch him from a distance, thinking that I might absorb a bit of his quiet concentration. I recognized that in comparison to Robert, I had been, and still was, a flighty butterfly ricocheting between the world of people and the world of my writing. His focused attention had clearly been honed through years of practice.

His cadence was measured, as though he were considering each step before committing to it, his feet going before the rest of his body. This gave him the appearance of moving at an angle, pulling himself along. If it rained or snowed, he added a pair of old-fashioned rubbers over his shoes, propped a tweed cap on his head, and wrapped an orange scarf around his neck. These were his only concessions to the weather.

I got to know Robert, to the extent that I could be said to know him, through our chance meetings on the street, though a brief exchange of glances was sometimes our only communication. I would remember his averted eyes, as if to suggest we both had more important business at hand than trading common pleasantries, when I returned home to my desk. When I lost faith in my writing, I thought of him next door at Connie's making his penny collections of poems. If he could carve such a unique and wonderful life for himself, surely I could keep writing despite the rejections and dubious prospects for publication.

In later years, I would wonder if it was simply the coincidence of my coming to live next door to Robert that made him accept my help, or if it was something that went deeper.

* * *

In the spring, the library was less crowded, and the damp smell lifted from the reading room, but I stayed home for my writing sessions, happy with the view of the pond and the sound of shrieking cats. On a day when, for the first time since back in October, I had thrown open all the windows, Clare came by to invite us to dinner. A few nights later, we walked up Whidden Street and around the corner to Franklin, another dead-end lane that went down to the pond.

We had not been at Clare's long when she darted into the living room and whispered, "Robert's here." Her eyes flashed a combination of alarm and amusement. It was clear that though she had invited him, she had not expected him to come.

Neighbors were there, and other writers Clare knew, many of them people who had lived in Portsmouth for years. I was talking with a man who restored antique houses when Robert entered the room with the gait that was familiar to all of us, his legs seeming to come first, his slight but elongated body next. He held a plastic cup of wine in his hand and looked us over in a way that could only be described as both casual and deliberate. I thought, as I had before, how he was the embodiment of slowness. He exuded a determination not to be rushed about anything, whether it was engaging in conversation at a party or making his way into town.

I went on talking to the restoration expert while Robert threaded through the assemblage to Jim's side. When I joined them a bit later, they were deep in a conversation about Linnaeus. Jim explained later that he had been talking about gardening, being unable to think what else he could discuss with Robert, and Robert had gone straight from growing vegetables to the botanical classification system Linnaeus developed in the 1700s.

"It was Strindberg, I believe, who said Linnaeus was a poet who happened to become a botanist," Robert said. "There's a certain poetry to classification. It's even musical in its way, you could say. It's hard to imagine the world without it." Robert let out a long and meditative *hmmm*. "He's rather shaped our way of thinking, hasn't he?"

Between the softness of his voice and my lack of acquaintance with the topic, I missed some of the facts about Linnaeus's life Robert went on to give us. I tried to look intelligent, as if I were following him with ease, though I was mostly trying to fish up anything I could recall from my high school biology class. Robert shifted the conversation to poetry, making reference to Chaucer and others I did not know. He tossed out names that sounded German and French and seemed to have circled back to Linnaeus. I was having trouble hearing him and following the thread, but clearly he had a sure grasp of these figures in literature and history and perceived a web of connections between their art and ideas.

I had the sense that night, as I would often in the future, that Robert knew everything there was to know about me before I said a word. With his still presence and needle-like gaze, he gave the impression of looking straight into a person, beyond the surface stuff that commonly defines us. There was no need to ask after ordinary affairs, like my work or Jim's, or where we had grown up. He seemed to have already divined anything of this sort that was of interest and rejected it for a glimpse into our very souls.

Robert finished his glass of wine and left before the food was served. The group of people in the kitchen parted for him as though making a path for a visiting celebrity. Once he was gone, a ripple of relief went over the crowd. People seemed freer then, more themselves, speaking loudly about TV shows and property taxes. The burden of engaging with a mind like Robert's was lifted from us.

"He's read a great deal," I said to Jim as we made the short walk home.

"He has," he agreed.

We fell into silence after that, and in the silence I recognized a shared understanding: We had typecast Robert and underestimated him. We felt slightly ashamed, but also pleased, in the way you are when something unexpected of the best sort happens, to have been wrong.

* * *

Downtown Portsmouth was home to seven bookstores in the early 1990s. In those days before the advent of the digital revolution, one used bookstore took up two stories in a rambling old house near the library. To find what you were looking for, or just to browse, you traveled through a warren of little rooms, up short flights of stairs and down others. Entire rooms were devoted to cookbooks and photography books, history and archaeology.

Another used bookstore occupied a cavernous storefront on a street near the river. Books sat in towers on the floor in this shop, and in the dim lighting, I had to peer at the spines to make out the titles. The place smelled of dust, a not entirely unpleasant odor. A cousin of Robert Frost's worked there on the weekend. He was a robust, red-faced man who wore a tweed jacket and vest and was always engaged in conversation with someone who had stopped by to visit. I delighted in seeing him perched on a stool behind the counter, a link to past times and to one of the first poets whose work I had truly absorbed and loved.

A third store, The Little Professor, sold new books out of a long space on Congress Street with aisles so narrow, it was a challenge to peruse the shelves. I made my regular stops here, too, to purchase gifts and look over the books on the new titles table. I bought Robert's book of poems at The Little Professor one day shortly after the party at Clare's. It was time, I decided, to find out who he was.

The book was titled *quo, Musa, tendis?* (The Latin translation is roughly "where, Muse, are you going?" The British poet James Kenneth Stephen, a cousin of Virginia Woolf, published a collection of poems with this title in 1891.) A slim volume of fifty pages with a tan cover the shade of old-fashioned brown wrapping paper, Robert's book had been published by Peter Randall, a local Portsmouth publisher, in 1983. The copy I purchased was not signed, though Robert stopped in at the store often. Many of the poems were short, some only a single line, and many were quite funny. If I had expected a window into Robert's heart, I was disappointed. With a few possible exceptions, there were no confessional poems here, no heartfelt explorations of anything traceable to his experience. Robert was more apt to use the collective "we" than the confessional "I" or to address the reader through the second person "you." When his poems were delivered in the first person, he managed to create distance and closeness at the same time. He made his claims, if he made them at all, in a deflected voice.

Whimsy was present in good measure, and a knowing defiance, as if he were stating from the outset that he was not going to play the poetry game as it was defined by the elites of that world. He would not make the all too common mistake of taking himself, or poetry, too seriously. One of his short untitled poems summed up his stance:

> *I hear America singing. Sometimes*
> *it troubles me.*

But the poems had their tender and reflective moments, too. Robert was capable of making me stop in my reading, as though he had reached from the page and shaken me awake, yet he accomplished this effect without calling attention to it. The poems were characterized, most of all, by spareness. They were little vanishing acts, sleights of hand beautifully done.

> *Dawn again,*
> *and I switch off the light.*
> *On the table a tattered moth*
> *shrugs its wings.*
> *I agree.*
> *Nothing is ever quite*
> *what we expect it to be.*

The "About the Author" note at the end of the book read: "Robert Dunn, a graduate of the University of New Hampshire, lives in Portsmouth, New Hampshire. 'An apple picker, currently celebrating his salad days,' he has promised us a fuller biography upon publication of his seventh book." I had heard from Clare that Robert had picked apples at one time. For how long he had done this, or where, no one seemed to know, but it was the only job he ever referred to having, other than his present position at the Athenaeum.

I would discover, as I read his poems over the years to come, that apples were a recurring theme.

On the title page of the book the following disclaimer appeared: "1983 and no nonsense about copyright. When I wrote these things they belonged to me. When you read them they belong to you. And perhaps one other."

Could Robert actually give up the copyrights, letting the poems go like unclaimed children? As an unpublished writer, other than a few stories in literary magazines, I was obsessed with the concept of copyright. Robert's cavalier approach alarmed and impressed me. Truly, it appeared, he was free of any sense of his worth as a public person. I could not begin to fathom that sort of freedom, hungry as I was for recognition of any sort.

Facing the title page was a list of acknowledgments that began with the enigmatic phrase: "Some of these poems happened in . . ." Robert could not bring himself to describe his poems as "published." The poems were happenings, pieces of street theater that somehow wound up on the printed page. With this introduction, he made it clear again that he would not participate in the farce of self-importance to which writers, poets perhaps in particular, are so prone. The publications listed in the acknowledgments included *Armadillo,* the *Beloit Poetry Journal, Contraband, The Lyric, Poems of the People,* and the *Portland Sunday Telegram.* The list trailed off with ellipses and the words: " . . . written on paper boats and airplanes . . . yelled from apple trees . . . whispered or sung softly on foggy nights to the deer and foxes."

I sat in my office looking out on Robert's house and read his book, delighted to find such a wry mind at work. In an age of what one of my teachers had called the "Macpoem," Robert's poems did not sound like anyone else's, except maybe Emily Dickinson's. He had the quirky precision of Dickinson, though his work tended to be lighter than hers, and less complex in its intention and effect. He was similar to Dickinson, however, in the pleasure he gave the reader in tracing an agile intelligence as it made startling, unpredictable turns. But Robert was not showing off for the sake of showing off. His poems were quick and unadorned, every word in service to the moment. The Robert I found between the covers of this little book wanted no one's solicitude or scrutiny. He had succeeded in disappearing and leaving the poems behind as the only evidence.

* * *

I became more determined after reading Robert's poems to speak with him when I saw him on the street. The time and place were key to this effort; if I passed him on Daniel Street on his way back to the Athenaeum in the middle of the afternoon, chances of a conversation were not good. There might be other people on the narrow walk, giving us nowhere to stand, and Robert might appear to be, uncharacteristically, on his way somewhere. If I met him in the lobby of the post office or the sidewalk outside, things might go better. Here he was more inclined to stop and entertain my questions, for that was often how the conversation felt, like a game of twenty questions.

"How is your next book coming?" I asked him one afternoon. These words, as I heard myself utter them, struck me as profoundly personal and probing, though if I had asked this of any other writer I knew, it would have been routine.

"It's moving closer," he said. He paused, eyebrows raised, as if to say, you know how it goes. "And you? How about your book?"

"I'm making progress."

His smile gave full confirmation of what we shared as writers. "It's quite amazing just how long it can take, isn't it?"

I nodded.

"But there's no need to hurry. No point to it, anyway, because the thing will take its own time no matter what you do."

With this oblique bit of encouragement, he pulled the brim of his cap lower, said good-bye, and walked off toward Market Square.

4.

Across the Pond

Portsmouth is shaped by water, the neighborhoods carved by tidal creeks and marshes and saltwater ponds. A map of town, covered in blue, gives an impression of land laid on top of the water, the streets an afterthought that hug one shoreline after another. The Piscataqua River, one of the fastest-flowing navigable rivers in the world, marks the northern edge of town and the boundary between New Hampshire and Maine. I often stop to watch the river rush beneath the Memorial Bridge, mesmerized by the power of all that water.

Three bridges span the Piscataqua. The Memorial Bridge connecting Route 1A from New Hampshire to Maine comes first. Next down the river is the Sarah Mildred Long Bridge on the Route 1 bypass, and just beyond is the grand arch bridge on I–95. When you look inland from the park by the river, you can see all three bridges telescoped, one after another, each one larger than the one that comes before. Along our working waterfront, there's the mountainous peak of the salt pile at a business that supplies much of the road salt for towns across New England and, beside it, another mountain of metal from scrapped cars.

In the other direction, away from the bridges, the Piscataqua runs out to the ocean. The inlets beyond Whidden Street mark the beginning of the meeting between river and ocean. Where exactly one ends and the other begins is hard to say, an apt metaphor for a town that wanders away from itself, twisting this way and that, as though unsure of its borders. Portsmouth is contained by its narrow streets and expanded by a sense of possibility, an openness to water and sky. It was this I loved first and loved most about the place.

When I stepped out the front door to retrieve the newspaper waiting there in the morning, I paused to take in the glassy surface of the pond or the exposed stretch of the mudflats, depending on whether it was high tide or low. The view never failed to still my mind for a moment. We had not chosen Portsmouth because it was near the ocean, but it fit a pattern in my life of living close to water. I was drawn to the silence and emptiness of those expanses.

One morning after I had checked on the state of the tides, I scanned the street for Zane, who as usual was up and out early. After a minute, he came trotting from around the back of Eleanor's house and zoomed past me through the door and on to the kitchen to finish his breakfast. I reached for the newspaper waiting on the stoop and saw a dispiriting headline: "J.J. Newberry's Closing."

Since 1928, J.J. Newberry's had been the place to go for feather dusters and grilled cheese sandwiches, suntan lotion and postcards, and a host of other items you didn't know you wanted or needed until you stepped through the door. When I walked into town to say good-bye, I discovered that the store's shelves had already been ransacked by bargain hunters. I bought boxes of gold Christmas balls for a dollar apiece and a tin tray decorated with instructions for dismembering a lobster for two dollars. The storefront sat empty for a number of months, a forlorn cavern, and then

The Gap moved in. Now blue jeans hung from a pole in the plate glass window, disembodied legs dancing alone, an advertisement for all that was trendy and cool.

The last grocery store downtown, an A&P with shelves full of canned goods that looked like their expiration dates might have passed, closed a short time later. Our neighbors in Connie's house next door did not have a car and, like most of the public housing residents, had nowhere left within walking distance of downtown to buy groceries and toiletries. The lack of grocery store did not seem to pose a problem for Robert, who lived on cigarettes, coffee, and sandwiches purchased at Richardson's, the remaining convenience store, but Connie took to asking neighbors for rides or got Ed to borrow one of our cars and drive her to the supermarket on the outskirts of town. The couple who lived on the other side of us began leaving the keys to their truck under its front seat. Ed could often be seen driving the truck in and out, until the neighbors sold the truck and bought a new car they were unwilling to loan out.

A few times I encountered Connie laden with grocery bags, making her cautious way down Pleasant Street, and stopped to give her a ride. It was only when I asked that she admitted she had walked all the way to the Pic 'n Pay out at the edge of town.

After just a couple of years, I could hardly be said to be "from" Portsmouth. I had heard lifelong residents joke that they were only third generation, still considered newcomers by the true natives whose ancestors arrived in the 1600s. Even so, the loss of J.J. Newberry's and the A&P were like wounds, signs of change in a place I had come to feel belonged to me. Jim and I had moved to Portsmouth at a moment when it was poised between the rough past of a waterfront lined with bars and brothels, and a gentrified future. The first waves of gentrification had occurred in the 1970s and '80s, but the pace of "improvement" had slowed with the recession of 1990 and 1991. Now, in 1992, the economy was beginning to recover, and relics like Newberry's were being swept aside. I joined the chorus of natives bemoaning the developers who were in the process of destroying the gritty charm of our city, despite the fact that I was part of the wave of new residents myself.

* * *

When I lived out in Provincetown in the late 1980s, in the years before I met Jim, I often went two or three days without speaking to anyone. Silence was at the heart of the time I spent in this outpost at land's end, yet I had the comfort of the funky little town around me, with its two thousand souls who waited out the winter, though the number often felt more like two hundred. Surrounded by the bay and ocean, and so sparsely populated in the off-season, the place seemed entirely forgotten with its shuttered shops and restaurants. Beyond town were miles of beach and dune, vast spaces where I could walk for hours without encountering anyone other than the gulls and foxes. I got to know a few people and traded conversation with the man who sold me a *New York Times* at the newsstand and the librarian who smiled when I checked out a new stack of books. In the afternoons, I rode my bicycle out to the beach, sometimes riding from one end of town to the other on Commercial Street without passing anyone. I loved the sense that I had fallen so far off the map, no one could find me. Provincetown was a place where I could live on the edge of human society, a part of it but apart from it, and this it seemed then was what I wanted.

As I watched Robert meander around downtown, it struck me that Portsmouth was a similar sort of place for him, where he could be surrounded by people and alone at the same time. Gradually I came to understand, though, that he was not really the recluse I had at first taken him to be. The writers I met all knew Robert and saw him regularly at poetry readings. He interacted with a good number of people each day in his travels downtown, stopped to talk with people on the street and with the shopkeepers, and drank coffee at Ceres Bakery with friends from the Athenaeum. Somehow he made the balancing act of being solitary but connected look easy.

I admired the nimble grace with which Robert navigated this territory, his ability to maintain a guarded privacy while, in a limited fashion, letting people in. He appeared to have mastered something fundamental I wasn't sure I ever would, though I was feeling my way toward my own kind of balance. For the first time, I appeared to have found a place to live where my warring impulses could coexist, and in my marriage a relationship that could accommodate, though not always easily, my need to disappear.

* * *

From the start, Portsmouth struck me as being in between town and city, with its packed streets and urban feel downtown, and its views of water along every edge. The back alleys have a city's look, and there are plenty of bars and cafés, plenty of places to go. With its city government, a population just over 20,000, and enough restaurants to seat every resident on the same night, it's not a postcard New England town. Still, there's an economy of scale to Portsmouth that suggests a smaller place, intimate and easy to know.

The Athenaeum, in Market Square a half block from where Newberry's had been located, remains the heart of old Portsmouth, a place that has remained largely unchanged since its founding in 1816. Like many residents, I was intrigued by the private library and its history. On a Thursday evening, Jim and I climbed the stairs to the third floor of the library in hopes of learning more about it. Rows of folding metal chairs waited in neat lines with a carousel slide projector on a small table in the aisle between them. It wasn't until we stepped into the room that I noticed Robert behind a desk off to the side. He got to his feet when he saw us and came over to say hello. There was no charge for the talk on the historic houses of Scotland, so Robert was not there to take tickets, but he was a greeter of sorts. He seemed both surprised and pleased to find us in the inner sanctum of his domain, and we had a brief conversation in which he owned that the historic houses of Scotland was an interesting topic, but soon after the lights were lowered he slipped out the door.

We were among the youngest people in the audience that night, both the topic and the Athenaeum seeming to attract an older crowd. The function room was disappointing, a nondescript space with a low ceiling, but through a doorway I glimpsed the more expansive interior of the library, where gleaming wooden shelves packed with antique-looking books stretched to an impressive height. The speaker was Scottish and showed slides of National Trust houses and castles dating back to the 1400s, many of the images slightly blurred or yellowed, like something out of my parents' old slide collection. When the lights came up, Robert did not reappear.

This visit did not satisfy my curiosity about either the library or Robert's work there, though I learned from a brochure I picked up on the way out that the Athenaeum is one of fewer than twenty private libraries remaining in the country. Members of the Portsmouth Athenaeum are called "Proprietors." There are four hundred of them and another six hundred "Subscribers" awaiting openings to become Proprietors, something I gathered occurred only on the death of a Proprietor. A certain prestige and an interest in history seemed to be the attractions of belonging to this club. The library's purpose, the brochure stated, was "to retain its tradition of serving as a locus of convivial interchange and intellectual discourse; to collect and preserve materials relevant to the study of the history of Portsmouth and the Piscataqua region; and to make these materials available to its Proprietors, to scholars, and to the general public."

If you stand in front of the North Church and fix your gaze on the Athenaeum without looking at the stores on either side, it's possible to imagine a time when horse carts would have gone clattering by. The distinct architecture and feel of Market Square trace back to a series of fires that consumed the downtown. The town established a fire district after the Great Fire of 1813, with the commercial buildings that went up required to be made of brick rather than wood. Many of these beautiful Federal style structures with their red brick remain intact, and the Athenaeum, built in 1805 after an 1802 fire leveled Market Square, is a prime example.

Tall arched windows on the first floor and a door framed by panels of antique glass give the building the look of something out of a Dickens novel. The windows provide a view into a high-ceilinged reading room with a black-and-white checked floor and walls covered with portraits of imposing figures from past centuries. A few armchairs line the edges of the room, as though waiting to be drawn up to a table in the center on which newspapers lie neatly folded. The door is always closed and the room often empty, as this part of the library is not open to the public, and the main entrance is in an adjoining building.

The exclusive spirit of the Athenaeum did not seem to fit Robert, though I suspected he cared only about having access to all those books. When I asked other writers in town what he did at the library, they said they thought he was a custodian of sorts. He put the chairs out for the talks and was often found hanging around the room on the third floor where visiting scholars did their research. He collected the mail from the post office box and straightened the newspapers in the reading room. Someone told me that in years past, Robert had calling cards printed up on which he listed the address of the Athenaeum, followed by his name and title—"Chief Metaphysician." In a profile in the *Portsmouth Herald*, he was quoted as saying, "It is never easy to come up with a job title. I wanted to be the gardener, but we don't have a garden." His duties, he said, consisted of "tidying up." Later I would learn that Robert worked about fifteen hours a week and, although he was so frail he carried the wastebaskets down to the dumpster one at a time, served an important role by staying late in the day and locking up. Somehow he managed to exist on the meager earnings of this, his only job.

* * *

The house was not much to look at, a small Cape with faded aluminum siding in an ugly shade of muddy brown. A chain link fence topped with barbed wire surrounded the backyard, whose centerpiece was a precarious-looking pine almost one hundred feet high. The tree's massive branches blocked the light and the view of the pond. I cannot say I had imagined the house I might one day buy, because I had never really imagined owning a house, but surely this little box of a place with the unkempt yard was not it.

"It's not the house, it's the location," Jim said, echoing the old truism about real estate.

I couldn't argue with him on this point. The house was just across the pond in the South End, within walking distance of downtown, and it had a driveway with room for more than one car. After enduring the parking wars on Whidden Street, this had become a priority. Our musings about the house would have to remain theoretical in any case, because we couldn't afford it.

At night I would search for the lit windows of the house across the pond, yellow beacons glowing in the dark, and wonder if we would ever be able to buy anything in Portsmouth. In December, the FOR SALE sign came down. We assumed that the house had been sold and went forward with plans to buy a place once we came up with a little more money. We saved whatever didn't go to rent and utilities and groceries that winter. In May, the FOR SALE sign reappeared. The sellers had taken the house off the market for the winter, hoping for a rebound in the market come spring. The price was still beyond what any bank would loan us, but we went to look anyway.

The kitchen, with its knotty-pine paneling and wall oven, was straight out of the 1950s, though in fact the date on the house was 1961. The kitchen and most of the other rooms remained just as they were when the house was built. We had to look past the hideous green shag carpet and postage-stamp–sized windows to imagine what the place might become. Jim was better at this than I was.

Throughout the summer of 1993 we toured houses in the area. Many were in better shape and bigger, but none offered a view of the pond within walking distance of downtown. In August we learned that the sellers had dropped the price of what had become our dream house. Though it was still more than we could afford, we made an offer anyway, twenty thousand under the asking price, and the sellers accepted it, bowing to a real estate market that had not yet recovered. So we became the owners of an oddity in the center of the historic district, a 1961 Cape that needed plenty of attention. Neither of us had purchased anything more expensive than a car before. Signing a mortgage felt like a momentous and frightening step, an even greater commitment than getting married. This was the ultimate in being settled. I would no longer be able to give one month's notice and move out.

From our new place, we could see our old house at the end of Whidden Street with the little shack covered in lobster buoys and Connie's house beside it. Sometimes I would glance out the kitchen window at just the moment Robert stepped into the street in his old overcoat and funny hat, and watch him walk slowly away. He was a reminder, like the surface of the pond stretching into the distance, to stop for a moment. I might go weeks without encountering him, but Connie's house and the knowledge that he was inside it posed a question: Are you writing? Or perhaps, more to the point, are you listening? With his head cocked at a slight angle, Robert often seemed to be listening to a distant voice no one else could hear. His presence across the pond asked me to do the same—or at least to attempt it.

*　*　*

I was driving up to Maine every other week now to teach a writing class that lasted an entire morning, part of an arts program for students from five public high schools. On my way home from teaching one day, I stopped at the post office and found Robert inside. He asked what I had been up to. I told him I had just come from class. I was flush with excitement because it had gone well.

"We discussed a poem by Joy Harjo," I told him. "The students were amazing. They pointed out all sorts of things I hadn't thought of."

"Such as?" he said.

"Do you know Joy Harjo?" I asked.

I expected Robert to respond that he did not know Harjo, a contemporary Native American poet. I had the mistaken impression that he was primarily interested in dead Greeks and did not keep up with what was being published currently.

"I know her work," he said.

When I explained that the poem we discussed was "She Had Some Horses," he nodded and added, "That's quite a wonderful poem. So what did the students have to say?"

"They talked about how she subverted the clichéd phrases she uses, so they weren't clichés anymore. And how the end of the poem is about the fact that the things we love and the things we hate can turn out to be the same. But she's talking about more than that. She's talking about the history of her people."

"There's a lot of repetition in that poem, as I recall," Robert said.

"Yes. One of the students said the repetition was like history, the terrible things that happened over and over to her people."

"You have good students."

I smiled. "I do. They surprise me."

"Ah," Robert said, registering the full delight of being surprised, in any way, at any time.

We said good-bye, and he went on, out the door, as I took my place in line.

In the past when I had stopped to talk with Robert, I often felt that I was conversing with someone who was not in this world. I thought of myself as an ambassador bringing bits of news and lore to him, though he might not want the debris I gathered from television and a host of other sources (even if I was a reluctant and ambivalent consumer of popular culture, I was clearly in this camp, while he remained in a realm of his own making). On this day when we met in the post office, my sense of the dynamic changed. If Robert had read Joy Harjo, he was not nearly as culturally isolated as I had imagined.

In the years after we moved across the pond, my meetings with Robert, spaced weeks or months apart, were brief and unpredictable, delightful and tantalizing. Each encounter was like a small window, opened and quickly shut. I came to understand, among other things, how much he delighted in defying expectations. Just when I thought I might have pinned him down for a moment, he slipped away again.

5.

Things of the Mind and Spirit

Getting married and coming to Portsmouth seemed at the time like the next step. The next step toward what, I wasn't sure; these changes simply made sense as part of a dimly perceived progression of events that added up to the unfolding story of what I called my life. I had met a man who was different from the others, steady and dependable, ready to be with me. I didn't want to date him or move into an apartment with him. I wanted a relationship that felt fated and, even though I resisted the idea, permanent. Looking back, I can't say, however, that I envisioned much beyond packing our belongings into a U-Haul truck and a couple of months later getting married.

As much as I took to the town, I could not imagine when we came to Portsmouth that we would stay here not just for two years or five but possibly the rest of our lives. But I could not imagine remaining anywhere for the rest of my life then, because I could not conceive of my life in those terms. I was still rooted in the present of my thirties, when time and possibilities seemed limitless, and convinced that, like a cat, I had many lives left. Anything might still happen to me.

In 1999, when we had been living in Portsmouth for eight years, I was approaching my mid-forties, an age that brought with it a changed perception of time. I no longer believed I had quite so many years to play with, and in ways large and small, I was continually reminded of an odd achievement of stability: the leaves in the yard that needed to be raked each fall and the classroom of new students who arrived with them; the regular round of holidays and visits with Jim's parents and mine; the dinners with people who were now close friends. The hours for writing were part of this fabric, though I still struggled to make sure I got enough of them. I came and went to the writing, though, with other things if not always feeling settled, at least no longer in constant flux. A litany of anxious questions I had carried around with me for years fell away.

When I was asked to serve on the selection committee for the new Poet Laureate of Portsmouth, I realized that I had achieved another measure of stability. I was no longer the invisible writer hiding in her office on the second floor of a house on Whidden Street. I had become someone who was recruited to serve on committees and contribute to bake sales, a citizen of this place.

* * *

I took a seat in a classroom at the middle school along with the others who had arrived clutching folders full of poems. I knew most of them, at least by sight. We were a group of writers and artists, citizens and organizers, elected officials and teachers. Eleven poets had been nominated for the position of poet laureate, and our task was to choose from among them. Robert was one of the nominees. When the head of the board of the Poet Laureate Program told me that Robert had been nominated, we speculated about whether he would be willing to be considered. He indicated that he would "throw his hat in the ring," as he put it, and sent along a few poems typed on his manual typewriter. One of them was two lines long.

The Poet Laureate Program, a new arts initiative, was in its second year. Esther Buffler, a ninety-year-old with a big personality, a passion for poetry, and an impressive collection of hats, had served her term as the first laureate, and now it was time to pick the second. Esther had taken on the role of poet laureate with the enthusiasm of a cheerleader and set about becoming the public face of poetry in town. She spearheaded a project that produced a CD of local poets reading their work and presided over its launch party in her inimitable style.

Those of us on the selection committee who came together that spring day at the middle school had been instructed to determine our own method of arriving at a choice. The discussion began tentatively, but before long we settled on going around the circle in order, voicing our first and second choices. When it was the librarian's turn, he spoke decisively. "Robert Dunn is my first, second, and third choice. He already is the poet laureate of Portsmouth. We should make it official."

I knew the librarian as the one who always wore a tie. He brought a gravitas to the library that struck me, on a first encounter, as out of place in New Hampshire, land of the flannel shirt and untrimmed beard. I would not have envisioned him as Robert's champion.

I had gone into the meeting convinced that I would be fair and open-minded, but Robert was not my first choice. I feared he could not handle the public duties the job required. Because the Poet Laureate Program was young and unestablished, we needed to present poetry in the best light. Though Robert was gifted enough as a poet, he came with a certain unpredictability.

An older woman who was a matriarch of sorts among local poets voiced my concerns. "Do you really think he's up to the job? Robert is so . . ." She paused for a long moment, during which all of us seemed to join her in the search for a word that might capture him. She finally completed her sentence with the simple pronouncement, "Shy."

A discussion ensued about the nature of the position. Would Robert feel comfortable speaking in public? Would he be able to organize the sorts of events that were expected? I knew that behind these questions lay others—with Robert as laureate, would the program be able to raise the money it needed to continue? Would it become a permanent part of the town's art scene rather than a nice idea that fizzled out in a few years? The librarian waved one hand impatiently in the air. "He'll do fine."

Around the table I saw consternation and anxiety on the faces of my fellow committee members. I was guilty, like them, of wanting to go with a safer and more socially acceptable choice. I flushed with shame for all of us.

The librarian continued to make an impassioned case. Robert was known to everyone in town, he said, and he was without question an accomplished poet. He could manage what would be asked of him.

We went on to discuss the other candidates, a courtesy we felt they deserved, but it became clear that a new perspective was moving through the room. A sense of collective excitement hovered over us. We were, it appeared, going to do something just a tiny bit daring. When we took the vote, it was unanimous for Robert.

* * *

A week before the formal announcement, I received a phone call from a member of the board of the Poet Laureate Program. "We were wondering if you would introduce Robert at the ceremony at City Hall," she said. "You know him better than any of us."

I said I would be happy to introduce Robert, though I was perplexed by her characterization of my relationship with him. By now I was familiar with most of the writers in the area. Many of them, I discovered, had known Robert since the late 1960s, when he first lived in Portsmouth, or even earlier, when he was a student at the University of New Hampshire. They had told me of seeing him at readings over the years, and buying his penny books, and stopping to have coffee with him when they ran into him by chance. Surely they knew him better than I did, or at least had a longer history with him.

I puzzled over this as I prepared my introductory remarks. I had come to feel that Robert was more comfortable with me than he had been in my first years in Portsmouth. He would stop to talk with me now, but these brief, enigmatic conversations on the street remained our only contact. If this was what it meant to know Robert well, what did his interactions with others consist of? Still, I felt a responsibility to be the person the occasion called for, one who could speak about him in a more personal way.

When the other writers in town learned that Robert was my next-door neighbor, they would give me surprised looks and ask, "Where does he live?" They had never been to the room he rented on the second floor of Connie's house; they did not even know that he rented a room there. For decades, they had refrained from asking how Robert managed his delicate existence, and he did not enlighten them. When they wanted to invite him to a poetry reading, they called the Athenaeum and left a message, or sent a written request well in advance, since Robert did not have a telephone. The fact that I was familiar with where Robert lived, though I had not visited him in that upstairs room myself, conferred a certain status on me. I knew more about him, or at least something more crucial, than others.

Robert arrived early at City Hall for the ceremony. I stood in the vestibule, outside the City Council chambers, feeling expectant and proud and just the tiniest bit worried, not only about my remarks but about Robert's. He was wearing a brown corduroy blazer, and his pants, a pair of khakis, had a newish look to them. Beneath the jacket, a dashiki-like shirt of 1960s vintage billowed over his meager frame, the same tan color as his pants. The Nehru collar, trimmed with a strip of gold and blue embroidery, was utterly anachronistic. If anyone else had worn it, someone would have asked, "Where did you find that?" On Robert, the shirt had an odd dignity. I looked away, touched and chastened. So this was Robert dressed up.

Inside the chambers, we sat in padded seats covered in plush red upholstery. A good-sized crowd had come for the ceremony that preceded the town council meeting, including many local writers. The announcement had been kept a carefully guarded secret, and when the mayor read a lengthy proclamation, arriving at the revelation only at the end, an audible gasp went through the room as she pronounced Robert's name. It was clear that everyone, even those who had come to City Hall that night for the public hearing on the school budget, was stunned and thrilled with this choice. In my introduction, I recalled how Robert and I had first met over a cat stuck in a basement and then over poetry. He stepped up to the podium and accepted a small bronze carving of a plumed pen, the handing on of which signaled the official "crowning" of the new laureate, and then, as I sat down, began to speak. His voice was clear and unwavering, assisted by a microphone, though this was not all that made it strong. There was confidence in his tone and ease. He was, I realized, enjoying himself.

"It says a lot about Portsmouth that there are eleven good poets to choose from," Robert began, referring to the other nominees whose names had been read. "Well, ten anyway." After this gentle gibe at himself, which brought laughter from the audience, he continued. "It was a Maine poet who said it's not so important to be the center of everything as it is to be the center *for* everything, and I think Portsmouth manages to be that. Boston is still the hub of the universe, and they have our deepest sympathy. But people come from all over the world to walk through our old streets, and they come not so much looking for material things, though you can find most anything a reasonable person would want at Peavey's Hardware, but they come looking for things of the mind and spirit, and the more they take away with them, the better place we are. Because, though we don't come right out and say it, I think we all secretly know that Portsmouth is one of the good places in the world. And so it's a fine honor to take a turn as your poet laureate. Of course Esther Buffler will always be our first poet laureate, and Esther's a pretty tough act to follow. You may as well know the worst, so I'm going to read a poem now." With this introduction, Robert tipped his head back and did not read but recited the following:

> *Almost a whole day without making a fool of yourself*
> *Almost a whole day wasted*
> *Almost a strange wound in eternity*
> *They say the road to hell is paved with good intentions*
> *But do you know*
> *The road to heaven is just covered with goofer dust.*

His recitation of these lines that managed to be both poem and joke was vintage Dunn, with its adroit blending of the high and low, and pleasure in confounding expectations poetic and otherwise. He sat down to thunderous applause.

* * *

I received the invitation in the mail on a small printed card. The Trustees of the Athenaeum requested my presence at a Bloomsday celebration on June 16 in honor of Robert Dunn, the city's new Poet Laureate. A few weeks later, I walked into town on a bright and warm afternoon. The door to the Athenaeum's reading room stood ajar, and the place was filled with people and laughter. I caught the mood as soon as I entered. It mirrored the day outside—joyous and surprised—shot through with the happiness of celebrating something so clearly marked for celebration, with no tinge of ambivalence or regret. At last Robert was being recognized as he should be.

The people crowded together, plastic cups of wine in their hands, were mostly older, in their sixties and seventies and beyond. The men wore suits and ties, the women wool skirts and blouses and ropes of pearls. They had that look of solidity and money, of coming from old New England families and knowing just what to do at a cocktail party.

I had not been inside long when a woman approached me. "I don't think I know you," she said. "Were you invited to this party?"

Flustered and confused, not to mention insulted, I finally said, "I received an invitation in the mail. I'm a friend of Robert's."

"Oh," she said, as if this was not a particularly satisfactory answer. "Robert gave us a list of people to invite." After a pause, she added, "We're thrilled he's the poet laureate."

"Yes," I agreed before walking away.

I was not part of the very thin slice of Portsmouth's upper crust. It wasn't just my too casual pants and lack of makeup and jewelry. I was an unknown. I felt the way I often do at cocktail parties, eager to make a quick exit when no one is looking.

As I poured myself a glass of wine, I spotted a few people I knew, other writers who were no doubt here because Robert had requested they be invited. Surrounded by Athenaeum board member types who gestured and spoke animatedly, Robert stood in the center of the room with that knowing and bemused look on his face, a plastic cup in his hand.

A man stepped to the head of the table and clapped his hands. "May I have your attention, everyone? We'd like to make a little presentation."

The room went quiet. "As you all know," the man said, "we are gathered here to acknowledge our new poet laureate. It couldn't happen to a more deserving fellow. Here at the Athenaeum, we have always known how talented Robert was. Now everyone else will know, too. Robert, we would like to show you our esteem and the pride we take in your accomplishments with a few small gifts."

He beckoned Robert forward. After a moment, Robert stepped toward him, head tucked into his chest.

"We all know that Robert doesn't need a lot," the man continued. A ripple of laughter went through the crowd. "But we thought maybe this might be of use."

From a large paper bag stashed under the oval table, he produced a wrapped package. Robert gazed at it as though uncertain what to do. The man gave him a gentle nudge and whispered, "Open it."

The silence in the room was thick with anxious anticipation. Giving Robert a gift felt like such a forbidden act.

Robert pulled off the wrapping paper to reveal an oblong box with a picture of a portable CD player on it. While he gaped at the box, as though trying to make out what it was, the man said, "It's a CD player. And we've given you a gift certificate to the record shop so you can buy some CDs."

"Ah," Robert said, letting the word out like a long exhalation. "How nice."

Another gift was produced from beneath the table—a case of wine. Every laureate, the man said with a laugh, should have his wine. Robert smiled and said simply, "Indeed."

It was clear that Robert was pleased. In his characteristic mumble, he said, "Thank you. Thank you all."

Another man read a rhyming poem about Robert full of puns, and Robert recited one of his poems. After a burst of applause, people took up their conversations again and ate the last bits of crackers and cheese. I found a poet I knew by a bookcase against the wall. After talking with her and a couple of other people, I saw that it was time to go. The women were removing the empty plates from the tables and scooping up crumpled napkins. I looked around for Robert but could not find him. "Where did Robert go?" I asked the poet.

She jerked her head toward a narrow hallway leading away from the reading room. "Out back, smoking a cigarette."

It didn't seem right to leave without speaking to him. I made my way through the dark hallway, toward a square of yellow light, and into the alley behind Market Square. He was standing there by himself next to a dumpster, a lit cigarette between his lips.

"I just wanted to say good-bye," I said.

He took a last puff on the cigarette, dropped it to the pavement, and ground it beneath his shoe.

"It was a very nice party," I said.

He nodded.

"And you got nice gifts."

"Yes. I'm afraid I can't do much with the CD player, though. I don't have an outlet in my room."

I considered this for a moment. "You could get batteries for it."

"Batteries," he said, as if I had named some wondrous invention. "I hadn't thought of that." He stepped forward, looking as if he might suddenly tip over, and I realized he was a bit drunk. "Ah, Katie, isn't this wonderful?"

The gesture he made, raising his slim fingers, seemed to indicate the blue sky overhead, the empty alley strewn with trash, and the party still going on inside. He continued to move toward me. I could not think what he was doing, until he reached out and grasped me in a loose hug. I stood there like a pillar, accepting the embrace, too startled to react and fearing that we were both about to land on the pavement. Robert regained his footing and stepped away, as unnerved, it appeared, as I was by what he had done.

I had never seen Robert hug anyone and, as it turned out, I never would again. He was not one for touching. The affection he expressed was more cerebral, conveyed through conversation and the play of words. That day I had a glimpse of a man who was capable of reaching out, who might even long for physical contact.

I treasured Robert the way many people in Portsmouth treasured him, as someone who helped to make our town unique and, walking the streets as he did, gave them character. I loved our conversations and the way he made me laugh. He clearly enjoyed people and could be a lively companion when he chose to be, but much of the time he chose solitude, and I respected this. That our brief encounters might spill over into a more personal relationship did not occur to me, just as it did not occur to others who knew Robert, because he did not seek out such relationships. Even in the blurry happiness of that afternoon, his hug was so unexpected that I did not know what to make of it. I said good-bye and quickly threaded my way back through the alley.

II.

Public
Versus Private

6.

The Pigeon Lady

I arrived a few minutes before seven to discover that I could barely wedge myself into the small space of the café. Every seat was taken, every table full. The crowd ranged in age from a group of teenagers to a number of people in their eighties. The high school students sat on the floor; others were pressed against the counter where the espresso machine whirred, or camped on plastic milk crates against the walls. The room was flush with a heat that carried not just the scent of human sweat but shared anticipation, excitement, and pride.

Nancy, the chair of the Poet Laureate Program board, moved from table to table like the matriarch at a Thanksgiving feast. "Did you have any idea?" she said when she reached my spot just inside the door.

"No," I said.

"They're more than sixty people here."

We traded amazed looks, and she went back to pushing her way through the crowd.

I had never heard Robert give a reading before, except for his presentation at City Hall, and as he placed himself behind the microphone, I felt like a nervous parent at the school play. He looked frail in his baggy corduroy pants and sweater vest, his thin frame made thinner by the crowd surrounding him. When he began speaking, he gazed up at the ceiling as though addressing its blank face. His words came out muffled; the microphone did not do much to amplify his hushed voice. He didn't look nervous. On the contrary, he seemed to be in his element, certain of what he had to offer. He simply appeared to be physically incapable of speaking more loudly.

In the packed room, we became one, every person leaning forward, perfectly still, in an effort to understand the words that drifted from him like wisps of smoke. We seemed to be giving him a silent, collective push, willing him to speak louder. I caught only a bit of what I gathered was an introduction. When he went on talking, I thought he was still positioning the poem to come, but then I realized that no, this was the poem, recited from memory. It was only then that I noticed he had come to the microphone with nothing in his hands.

I caught the thread of the poem, isolating one word and then another. I remembered this one, vaguely, from *quo, Musa, tendis?*, though it seemed like a different poem in Robert's voice, alive in an utterly wonderful and more whimsical way.

Public Notice
They've taken away the pigeon lady,
who used to scatter breadcrumbs from an old
brown hand and then do a little pigeon dance,
right there on the sidewalk, with a flashing
of purple socks. To the scandal of the
neighborhood. This is no world for pigeon
ladies.

There's a certain wild gentleness in
this world that holds it all together. And
there's a certain tame brutality that just
naturally tends to ruin and scatteration and
nothing left over. Between them it's a very
near thing. This is no world without pigeon
ladies.

Now world, I know you're almost
uglied out, but . . . just think! Try to
remember: What have you done with the
pigeon lady?

Robert recited his poems for maybe eight minutes, a space of time that felt both longer and shorter than it was. It was nearly impossible to tell where one poem left off and the introduction to the next began. He did not take pains to "deliver" his poems the way other poets might, with the adoption of a falsely poetic cadence that often sounds forced. He spoke the poems as though they were part of a conversation. The language and rhythm in which he talked and the voice of his poems were one and the same. I recognized this as a testament to his mastery of the art of both poetry and life.

Hearing Robert recite his work was a revelation in more ways than one. He was not attempting to "do" anything with his poems. He was not trying to make them "be" something. I had read his work on the page and admired it. I heard the poems differently, though, when they came with his slight voice. They struck me that night as having the quality of found objects he had stumbled on and managed to preserve, whole and unsullied. He had not gotten in the way of these discoveries. His ego was largely absent from the words and the form they took, and from his shy yet generous recitation of them.

How far I was from achieving anything like this, in the words I wrote and in the way I felt about them.

Robert presided over a number of projects during his two-year term as poet laureate. The institution of a monthly poetry reading, dubbed the Poetry Hoot, was the first of these. We were gathered that night for its launch, which presented two featured poets followed by an open mic. After a somewhat sustained campaign, the members of the board had persuaded Robert to be one of the featured readers at the first Hoot along with Esther Buffler. He had not disappointed us.

* * *

I saw Robert more often since he had been named poet laureate. He had been featured in various local newspapers and seemed to be making an effort to live up to a public role. He showed up for readings besides the Poetry Hoot and other arts events around town. I ran into him more frequently as I did my errands, and we had more to talk about when we stopped on the sidewalk.

One afternoon I encountered Robert as I passed through Market Square. This day he came toward me on the brick walk, head raised, eyes lively, and called out hello before I had a chance to speak. I returned the greeting with the sense that being so publicly acknowledged by him represented a breakthrough of some sort.

He withdrew the hand sunk in the pocket of his trench coat and held it toward me. It took a moment for me to realize there was something there, in the palm of his hand, that looked like a square of yellow paper.

"I have that book for you," he said.

What book, I thought. "Your poems?" I said, comprehension dawning on me. He nodded in the affirmative. I took the small book from his hand. It had the handwritten title "Watching the snow" across the top with a little block print of a snowflake-like design beneath. Under this was simply "Robert Dunn."

"What do I owe you for this?" I asked.

He gestured toward the book, indicating I should turn it over. On the back cover, off to the side, was the notation 1 cent. I felt, for the first time with Robert, something like annoyance. I did not intend to give him a penny. I fished in the pocket of my jacket and found a five-dollar bill.

"Oh, dear," Robert said. "I'm afraid I don't have change for that."

"I don't want change."

"No, no." He curled his fingers closed in a gesture of refusal. "If you don't have a penny, you can give it to me another time."

"How about a dollar?" I took out another bill.

He pulled back the hem of his coat and extracted a collection of coins from the front pocket of his corduroy pants. I watched as he counted out pennies and nickels and quarters.

"I don't want the change," I said.

He ignored me.

"Robert, really, keep the change."

He didn't raise his head. When I persisted, he agreed to accept a quarter from me. I would have paid him twenty dollars for the book if I could have, but this transaction, like any with Robert, would happen on terms he dictated or not at all.

I went on to the post office, and he crossed the street to the Athenaeum, leaving me amazed, as he often did. I had not quite believed he actually sold his little books for a penny. As I made my way home, I remembered the expression of pure delight on his face when he extended his hand with its small offering and wished I could embrace that sort of delight myself more easily. My initial reaction was that the transaction had felt all wrong; in my giving him so little money, he had forced me to adopt his standards, financial and otherwise.

This was the genius and beauty of his penny books, but how confounding and humbling I found the experience, how much it asked me to reconsider my understanding of being a writer.

* * *

The announcement appeared in the *Portsmouth Herald* and caused consternation all over town. Richardson's, the old-style family grocery and convenience store on State Street, was closing after fifty-two years. For as long as anyone could remember, two generations of Richardsons had manned the cash register from seven in the morning until well after midnight three hundred and sixty-five days a year. In the newspaper article, Basil Richardson boasted that he had never closed, even on Thanksgiving and Christmas, when he kept a few turkeys on hand for those who hadn't made it to the supermarket or found themselves with an unexpected influx of relatives.

I would stop at Richardson's to pick up a quart of milk or a stick of butter, last-minute items forgotten at the supermarket. These purchases were often made at night on the way home from a concert or a dinner out, when it suddenly occurred to me we were missing an essential ingredient for breakfast. This was when things got lively at Richardson's. Rowdy groups of teenagers gathered on the sidewalk outside waited for an emissary to return with beer. Inside, tough-looking characters rubbed coins against scratch tickets and were reprimanded by the clerk for lighting up cigarettes before leaving the store.

There was considerable angst in Portsmouth over the closing of Richardson's, especially on the part of those who seldom entered the place. Richardson's was the last of a nearly extinct breed—the family-owned store that had been part of town for as long as anyone could remember, slightly seedy but always dependable. When I heard the news, I lamented the passing of Richardson's like everyone else, but I was even more concerned about Robert than I was about the gentrification of our unique city. The cup of coffee and premade sandwich he purchased at Richardson's each evening pretty much made up his complete daily diet.

When I saw Robert shortly after the store closed, I brought up the tragedy that had befallen Portsmouth in the aghast tone everyone else had been using. He smiled and said, "We wouldn't want things to stay the same just for the sake of staying the same, now, would we?"

This quick jab, a quip he let stand alone without elaboration, was another challenge to common thinking, mine and everyone else's. I heard the implicit message behind it. Nothing could be controlled or predicted, and the sooner I saw my way to accepting this, the happier I might be.

Robert recognized that change was inevitable while understanding that it made no difference, not to what really mattered. The shining of light through language on the darker corners of human existence was what was important. Literature with the power to move and instruct people, to comfort them and make them laugh, to illuminate the beautiful and horrible, stood outside time. The rest was essentially gossip.

By the spring of 2000, when Richardson's closed, property values (and property taxes) had soared, and Portsmouth was regularly showing up on lists of the country's ten most livable small cities. Despite the influx of chain stores and the loss of icons like J.J. Newberry's and Richardson's, Portsmouth retained hints of its old character. Because of the military bases located here, Portsmouth has always been more diverse than other places in New Hampshire, and it has long been a Democratic stronghold in a state traditionally known for a quirky brand of libertarian Republicanism. The Air Force base closed in the early 1990s, but we still have the Portsmouth Naval

Shipyard, which is located on an island in the river. We still have the fishing wharf near Strawbery Banke where the commercial boats bring their catches each day, and the great salt piles on the riverfront downtown and the mountain of scrap metal at the business next door. Tankers bring the salt from Chile and Peru and take away the scrap metal, and their crews from countries all over the world visit the bars.

There was no denying, though, that much of what made the town unique and interesting, especially to the artists and musicians who were rapidly moving out because they could no longer afford to live here, was being transformed. As usual, Robert had his distinct take on the matter. There was no sense in opposing change simply for the sake of opposing it.

* * *

On a late afternoon in the spring, a year after Robert was appointed poet laureate, we stood on the deck of an old tugboat that had been turned into a restaurant and moored just beneath the Memorial Bridge. We were there to celebrate the unveiling of Robert's public art project. He had come up with the idea, which was executed by the Poet Laureate Program board, to place poems in public places around the city with the aim of reaching people who might not know they were in need of poetry and, if only for a moment, surprise them, maybe convert them. A poem by Jane Kenyon, anchored under plexiglass, now decorated the wall inside the parking garage. With persistence and some difficulty, the board had persuaded Robert that one of his poems should go public, too. Robert's poem hung on a fence below us, near the tugboat's mooring, a spot where walkers might pause to look out over the river. It read:

From here you can see the tide
Turn like a door on its hinges:
We're just going out. Do you want
Anything from the ocean?

A small group of us had gathered for wine and cheese and crackers. It was a warm day with not much wind, and as I gazed out at the fast-moving river, with Robert standing beside me, I thought how lucky we were to be perched above the waters of the Piscataqua with the sun bathing our faces.

Robert sipped his wine and, as usual, did not say much. He stared off at the opposite shore—Kittery, Maine—with that sage-like expression on his face. When someone in the group surrounding us mentioned a movie they had seen about the Catholic activist Dorothy Day, he turned his head. The conversation moved on to other topics after a moment. Robert let the talk go on and then, when the others were engaged in their conversation, leaned toward me and said quietly, "I knew her, you know."

"Knew who?" I said.

"Dorothy Day."

"You knew Dorothy Day?"

"Yes. She was a formidable woman." He turned back toward the river as though that was all that needed to be said.

"How did you know Dorothy Day?" I asked.

"I lived in New York. I spent a lot of time at the Catholic Worker."

I had never heard of Robert living anywhere but New Hampshire. It was difficult to picture him walking the streets of Manhattan. "When did you live in New York?"

"The 1960s."

"And what did you do at the Catholic Worker?"

"I helped out at the soup kitchen. I was living on the Upper West Side, by Columbia, but I went down there to the Bowery quite a bit. It was a rather rough part of town then."

"What was Dorothy Day like?"

"A force to be reckoned with."

This tantalizing glimpse of Robert's past was all I would get. He finished his wine and turned to someone else. Clearly he was proud of having known Dorothy Day, and I sensed he took a secret delight in dropping this revelation at my feet, as if to say, "There are many things about me you don't know."

Robert had made a life that was both hidden and transparent. His daily routine was so circumscribed that it was impossible to imagine him outside his regular routes, but with our conversation on the deck of the boat, Robert appeared to be suggesting that I, and the rest of those present, did not know him at all. He wasn't going to let us get to know him, either, though he would parcel out little hints. I went home and told Jim, "Robert knew Dorothy Day." The information was notable enough to repeat, though it didn't, on a second telling, amount to much.

7.

Dancing on the Head of a Pin

‟What happened to the pond?" a friend visiting from Kansas said in alarm. She had arrived the day before when the water was high and now stood gazing out the kitchen window at the mud flats, her face pulled together in puzzled wonder.

I explained that the pond was a tidal body of water that emptied and filled again every six hours.

"But where does the water go?"

"Out to the river and on to the ocean."

"And then it comes back?"

I smiled, amused by her amazement. "Then it comes back."

"How do you get anything done?" she said. "If I lived here, I'd spend all day watching the water go in and out."

I do watch the tides, though half the time I'm barely aware I'm doing so. The shifting tides are simply a piece of the view, like a clouded or sunlit sky. I take note of the state of the water and forget it a moment later.

The dining room table, where I sometimes sit to write, has a view of the backyard and the pond. Some days I am staring at a blue stretch of water as I search for the right words; other days it's a cratered sea of mud. Both have their beauty, making a space at the foot of the lawn that has no other purpose. This would be news to the gulls and ducks and herons who forage for food there, but in my human world, the pond seems to be there simply to rest the eye. The water can't be built upon or walked across. How few things in modern life bring us back to beauty and nothing else.

I made my forays to the library in our first years in Portsmouth to work surrounded by the hushed hum of activity there, but now I cherish the feeling, when I can find it, that I am the only person for miles. The pond, an oasis of silence, gives me that. Dotted with rocks and bits of driftwood, the mud flats are ribboned at low tide with the last traces of water, a map scored into the muck. The imperceptible movement of small streams mirrors the path of the writing. I cannot see where it is headed, and the words may ebb away completely, but I know they will return.

Jim and I often marvel that we came to Portsmouth when we did. How lucky we were to have arrived before Portsmouth had been fully discovered and property values skyrocketed. Our timing, purely by accident, had been right. My timing with the writing was another matter. I followed my own internal clock, oblivious to the trends in bookselling and marketing, and to the dire predictions that in a few years no one in America would be reading at all. I clung to the writers I loved and read for inspiration, revised the pages and revised them again, and at last the novel that had dogged, eluded, and consumed me for so many years was finished. I had sent earlier drafts of the book out to agents and editors with no success. Now, after another rewrite that involved throwing away an entire plot line and adding a couple of new characters, the book was accepted by an agent and another waiting game began. When I sat at the dining room table writing that second year of Robert's tenure as poet laureate, I would look up from the computer screen and check on the status of the tides, and glance at his house across the pond. The stillness of the scene helped me stay focused on the questionable enterprise of a second novel while the first one racked up repeated rejections.

* * *

We had lost J.J. Newberry's and Richardson's, but we still had Peavey's Hardware downtown. A sign with the store's hours hung on the front door, one of those printed forms you might buy at a store like Peavey's, with blank spaces where the hours can be filled in by hand. In each of these blank spaces, Monday through Saturday, the numbers 9–5 appeared in wobbly writing. Beside Sunday were the words "Go to church."

Peavey's occupied a small space in an old building on Market Street. Pressing the antique latch and opening the door, I had the feeling of entering someone's living room. The store's shelves, crammed with stuff arranged in a fairly idiosyncratic fashion, reinforced the impression of a unique place that catered to the equally unique individuals who shopped there. In this, it had a distinctly New Hampshire flavor. For better and worse, this is a state that has taken the value of individualism to extremes. Our state motto is, after all, "Live Free or Die." A trip to Peavey's always felt like something of an adventure. For such a small store, and a family-run one at that, it could be difficult to find what you were looking for. That individualism thing again. In New Hampshire, it's understood that if someone doesn't ask for help, you don't presume they need it. I often wandered around Peavey's for a good ten minutes, which gave me time to peruse all the wonderfully old-fashioned items the store carried that you might not find elsewhere—egg timers and gingham-checked aprons, canning labels with floral borders, and wooden rulers of the sort people used to have on their desks. Peavey's carried the more standard stock, too, like nails and paintbrushes and duct tape. I would stop in for birdseed when I ran out of it and didn't want to drive out to Home Depot.

For years, when Jim and I had out-of-town visitors, we would take them past Peavey's and point out the sign on the door with its barked instruction to "Go to church" on Sunday, a telling anachronism that never failed to elicit bursts of laughter. Robert was a fan of Peavey's, recognizing it as a quintessential New Hampshire business, though I can't say I ever saw him go into the place. When the store closed, ending a run of more than two centuries of similar businesses in that location (the first hardware store there was opened in 1786), we noted its passing in a brief and slightly mournful exchange and moved on. The owner had worked at Peavey's for sixty-three years. It was the last of the hardware stores left downtown, and everyone knew it would not be replaced. A clothing boutique took over the space a short time later.

* * *

I entered the wood-paneled room in the basement of the Methodist church and found Robert seated in a voluminous easy chair that nearly swallowed him up. His canvas shoulder bag lay on the floor at his feet. That fall I had been asked to serve on the board of the Poet Laureate Program. We met on the second Wednesday of the month at four o'clock in the space donated by the Methodists. I understood that the poet laureate was not required to attend the monthly meetings and was surprised to find Robert present. I wondered how he had gotten to the church before realizing that of course he had walked. It was not that far from downtown, just a bit off his usual route. He was being paid as poet laureate the princely sum of $800.

This was substantial enough that he took his responsibilities seriously, though he would have no doubt taken them equally seriously had he been paid nothing.

Nancy told the board members how much money we had in the bank and how much we had received from our latest fundraising drive. Others reported on the sales of the CD and the writing of grants. Robert watched the proceedings with a familiar expression on his face, inscrutable and slightly mischievous. I imagined that he found these meetings tedious, full of bureaucratic nonsense, but when the talk turned to other matters, this did not seem to be the case.

I was to discover that when Robert spoke at board meetings, he spoke briefly but decisively. Often his observations consisted of no more than a sentence, and they frequently were delivered when everyone thought the discussion was finished. Invariably they sent us back to consider a point that was glaringly obvious, and of critical importance, though it had been overlooked by all of us.

Today Robert said simply, "I think we might want to do something for World Poetry Day."

Everyone in the room turned toward him as though they had forgotten he was present.

"World Poetry Day," Nancy said. "Well, yes, that sounds like a fine idea. What might we do?"

"I was thinking a reading might be nice," Robert said.

"A reading of the work of world poets?" another board member asked.

"That's a possibility of course. But I was thinking more along the lines of the international poets themselves. We're a bit insulated here in New Hampshire, don't you think? It might do us some good to hear from poets from other countries."

A lengthy pause followed this declaration. Robert was right, but where were we going to find these international poets? Hildy said that she knew a Haitian poet and a Turkish poet, both in New England. I offered my friend, a Russian poet, who was in Washington, D.C., but might be persuaded to make the trip. The conversation went on from there, until we had settled on applying for a grant so we could give the poets at least a small stipend. Robert slumped back in his chair and said nothing. He had set the thing in motion and was content.

The idea took on substance in subsequent meetings. We ended up with the poets originally proposed and another from Belgium, all of whom were currently living in the U.S. A couple of months later, when we were working out the details, Nancy suggested a church downtown as the venue.

"It's not accessible," Robert said.

"Accessible?" Nancy asked, uncertain, like the rest of us, she had heard him correctly.

"Wheelchair accessible. We can't hold an event in a place that's not wheelchair accessible."

Glances went round the room. The tone in Robert's voice was unyielding, almost combative. I had never seen him in this mood.

"Are there any other places downtown that are accessible?" Nancy asked.

Various people offered suggestions, but on further discussion, it was determined that none of them were.

"I won't attend if we hold it somewhere that isn't accessible," Robert said when we appeared ready to give up and go with one of the venues already mentioned.

At that meeting I saw in Robert a rigid adherence to principle I would encounter again in the years ahead. Someone was assigned to do research on this issue, and at the next meeting we agreed to hold the event at the Sheraton with its elevators for those who might need them.

* * *

The night of the reading, I offered to host a dinner at my house. Our Russian poet flew in from Washington, the Belgian and Haitian poets drove up from Boston, and the Turkish poet came from a nearby town in New Hampshire. Robert walked over from Whidden Street, arriving promptly at five-thirty. I had been afraid he wouldn't come to dinner and then once he accepted the invitation feared he would refuse any food, but he took a glass of wine and sat happily watching the poets in animated conversation around him. When it came time to eat, he filled his plate.

The night was not promising. A cold rain was falling, with a forecast for ice later, but at the function room at the Sheraton, we found a standing-room-only crowd of roughly a hundred and twenty-five people. Robert had hit on something significant. New Hampshirites recognized the rarity of this chance to hear poetry that might transport them to other places.

Robert could not be persuaded to make an introduction, but he sat in the second row looking pleased. The poets read in their original languages and in English. The variety of their work was startling, and the atmosphere in the room electric. Robert referred to the event on numerous occasions in the years to come, clearly proud of its success, though when we gave him credit, he would say, "Oh, I didn't do anything. I just had the idea." I would remember that night as the first and only time he came to my house.

* * *

"Go to church," the owners of Peavey's told us, and we laughed because it was such a throwback to a time when expectations of this sort might have defined our town. There's a Jewish temple just a couple of blocks from where Peavey's was located. They're not going to church on Sunday, nor are the Buddhists and Muslims, nor are all the people running road races, taking their kids to soccer games, and going out to brunch. But I do go to church, and in doing so, I am a rarity among my friends.

As a child, I attended church six days a week. My father is an Episcopal priest, and being in church so frequently did not seem unusual to me. Our life as a family revolved around the church; in many ways, our life was the church. From Monday through Friday, I attended chapel every morning at my Episcopal church school wearing a little green beanie we called a chapel cap. Sunday mornings my mother and sisters and I went to church at the seminary where my father was on the faculty or traveled uptown to the Cathedral of Saint John the Divine, where he moonlighted on the weekends as an extra priest. The typical preacher's kid grows up in the confines of a small-town church community, always on view and held up as an example. My childhood, spent on the campus of the seminary with two hundred young men studying for the priesthood, was something else entirely. I was freed of some of the burdens of being a preacher's kid and saddled with others, but I was undeniably steeped in the tradition and ritual of the church.

Religion, I discovered, was something else Robert and I had in common, though he would bristle at my use of this word that has come to stand for dogmatic belief and bureaucratic institutions. Our conversation about Dorothy Day was the first clue. Over time he let slip other clues in the same surreptitious way. I learned that he had attended Christ Church, the church to which I belong, and that he had a thorough knowledge of the Book of Common Prayer and the daily order of monastic prayers with its services like Compline. When I read one of my poems at the Poetry Hoot with lines that echoed the hymn known as "Saint Patrick's Breastplate," Robert sidled up to me afterward and said, "You know Saint Patrick took that from a Pagan chant. The Native Americans have a similar chant." He appeared to be one of the only people in the audience that night to recognize the reference to the hymn.

Christ Church was founded in the late 1800s as a mission of Saint John's, the wealthy, established Episcopal church in Portsmouth. From the start, Christ Church was dedicated to outreach to the city's poor, a legacy that still defines it. With its lack of pretense and working-class roots, Christ Church was the sort of place I could imagine Robert, but his references to religion were little pearls dropped at my feet hinting at a larger story that would not be told. That he might have been comfortable in the Episcopal Church, with the rich language of its Book of Common Prayer and restrained beauty of its rituals, made sense, though it was hard to imagine him standing around chatting with the congregation at coffee hour. I would learn later that he had not only attended Christ Church but lived in the rectory with a charismatic young priest and some other young men for four years in the 1960s, after he graduated from the university. This was not information Robert shared with me himself; he made only the most indirect and vaguest of comments about his time at the church. From longtime parishioners I learned that he used to place an apple rather than money in the collection plate.

In years to come, I would puzzle over this thread, another of the connections I appeared to share with Robert, and wonder if it was a reason he eventually turned to me for help more than others in his circle of friends. Did my association with the church make him feel he could trust me, even though he had no use for the church himself now?

* * *

When Robert was still serving his term as poet laureate, I became one of the editors of a literary magazine focused on art and faith. The magazine, now defunct, was published by a fairly conservative seminary on the west coast. I was recruited through an old college friend of Jim's. The seminary gave us a good deal of freedom, and though each issue of the magazine opened with a statement of faith, this statement was broad enough that I could live with it. The editors came from various religious backgrounds and were poets and fiction writers. We were excited about the possibility of bringing the slant of faith to writing and art, not in any doctrinaire way but as a lens that might sharpen and magnify both. This, it seemed, was a contribution to the arts world that might be different.

At one of the Poet Laureate board meetings, I gave Robert a copy of the magazine and asked him if he would like to contribute some poems. About a week later, an envelope arrived in the mail addressed to me in a beautiful script in black ink. Inside, I found the following letter written in the same precise but flowing hand on heavy, unlined paper.

Portsmouth, NH
January 22, 2000

Dear Katie,

A belated thank you for the Mars Hill Review. It's a pleasure to read about stuff that matters. So often literary magazines leave you with the feeling that much less needs to be said.

   However, I don't think that the kind of poetry I write would do for them. Of course we share some of the same con-cerns—the ultimate ones—but I would feel somewhat bogus if I tried to deal with them in religious language. There's a lot to be said for not taking the name in vain, you know. For one thing, it would cut down drastically on the number of sermons that get preached.

Mind you, I'm not casting nasturtiums on religious poetry as such—although I think we both wish that it could be held to a higher standard of excellence than we generally see. Well, perhaps Chesterton was right after all, and a thing worth doing is worth doing badly.

Incidentally, did you know that 301,655,722 angels (precisely) can dance on the head of a pin? Or could in the fourteenth century. I have not been able to find any recent quotations.

Cheers,
Robert

This letter, the first I had received from Robert, stung me, though I found it amusing at the same time. I did not think that we were publishing "religious poetry." I thought we were publishing poems that sometimes dealt with matters of faith and, even then, did so indirectly. Though couched in gentle cleverness, Robert's letter was a clear refutation of the effort we were undertaking in the magazine. He had put me on notice that he would sniff out any false attempts to impose "religious language" on the free spirit of poetry.

I had asked Robert to submit some poems because, first of all, I admired him as a poet. I also figured, wrongly as it turned out, that he would be pleased to have his work published in just about any literary magazine. I did not see his work as "religious" per se, though one could make the argument that his poems, with their resemblance to Zen koans, had their spiritual side. Our brief conversations about the church had led me to believe, again wrongly, that Robert would be sympathetic to the aims of the journal. But most of all, I saw myself as doing Robert a favor by offering to publish his work. That he didn't see it as a favor was the worst rebuke.

That winter large flocks of crows gathered over Market Square in the late afternoon and turned the tops of the trees black. They came to mind as I composed a postcard to Robert. I thanked him for his letter and made some vague expression of regret that he would not be submitting his poems, then closed with: "Have you seen the crows in Market Square recently? I don't think they're a sign from God, but I do think they deserve our notice."

I did not receive a response, but I hoped he had gotten my message. Whether you believe God has anything to do with those crows thronging the trees or not, they are a reason for awe, and isn't this, called by the name of God or not, the essence of God?

8.

The Room on the Second Floor

R obert finished his term as poet laureate in the spring of 2001. Just after Christmas that year, I arrived home one evening from running errands to find a box waiting by the kitchen door. There were no gifts from families or friends we were still expecting. This was a gift of a different sort, the first copies of my novel, in hardback with a bright, shiny cover. Once I had ripped open the box, I stood by the kitchen sink gazing at this thing in my hands. It did not seem real after so many years of dreaming of this moment, and at the same time, it was all too real. I was elated and terrified by the thought that my book would soon be on bookstore shelves.

The Little Professor had closed, and we had no bookstore downtown, so I gave a reading at Barnes & Noble in the mall at the outskirts of town. I had rehearsed thoroughly and felt ready, but I was not prepared for the crowd of more than a hundred waiting inside. The newspaper had done a feature article that week, and the book had gotten some nice reviews. My hometown crowd turned out to give the book a great send-off. If I needed proof of how thoroughly I had become a part of this place, the people gathered at the bookstore that day were confirmation of how far I had come from my wandering days.

After the reading, I took a seat at a table and signed books. This part of the event was fun but awkward, I discovered, a bit like being in a receiving line at a wedding. You want to have a significant exchange with all the people who have made the effort to be there, but there isn't time for more than a few words. I had been signing books for a good fifteen minutes when I looked up and found Robert in front of me. I had not seen him in the crowd when I was reading. He appeared like an apparition in his corduroy jacket and tweed cap.

"This is quite something," he said as he placed a book in front of me.

"Yes," I agreed.

The standard "best wishes" did not seem adequate as an inscription for his copy. Finally I settled on "For Robert, who watched from the house next door as I wrote this book." Later it occurred to me these words made him sound like some weird Peeping Tom.

Robert smiled and said, "Congratulations." Someone snapped a photo of us. He scooped up the book and said, "I'll let you get to your public," and then he was gone.

I hadn't sent Robert an invitation. I realized this with a start of guilt, but I had assumed he would not want to venture out to the mall. Afterward I asked several people if they had given him a ride. None of them had. We concluded that he must have taken the bus.

Robert appeared genuinely happy for me, and I was touched that he had somehow gotten to the bookstore on his own. As he had before, though, he startled me with his still gaze and those words—*I'll let you get to your public.* In Robert's faint mumble, the word *public* took on a damning cast, though his tone was playful. The public, his comment seemed to imply, was not what I should care about, as

I so clearly did at that moment. The writing, not any public response to it or estimation of it, should be my only concern.

As Robert turned away, leaving me to face a line of people waiting to have books signed, I felt that he had seen through me to the deep need for approval, the great strivings of ego, that lay at the heart of my desire to publish a book. Only by divorcing myself from the hunger for affirmation, his quip suggested, would I find what I truly desired. This is what he wanted for me, what he wanted for anyone who wrote.

A month later I came out of the bank one afternoon and encountered Ed lumbering through Market Square. I had not run into him downtown in some time, a year or more. He barked out my name as he always did and said, "That was a good book."

I gave him a puzzled look.

"The book you wrote. I read it. It was damn good. Connie's reading it now." He snapped out this pronouncement and went on his way.

I returned home humbled by the thought of my book being passed from Robert to Ed to Connie. If I hadn't fully understood before the magic of sending a book out into the world, I understood it now. A piece of me had become part of that unique household. I felt chastened, too. Robert had presumably read my book and then shared it. Perhaps the implicit critique I had heard in his remark at the book launch was not only that. Perhaps it contained some admiration as well.

* * *

Robert had never looked well. The fact that he weighed next to nothing was a given and had been the case as long as anyone could remember. He had the skin of someone who has spent little time in the sun and has smoked a pack of cigarettes, or more, every day for years. His teeth were in dismal shape, some of them missing, with those that remained darkened or yellowed nubs. To describe a lump on someone's head as resembling an egg has become a cliché, but the one protruding from Robert's forehead was truly the size and shape of one. I wondered if it was a tumor, some sort of a growth that would surely kill him, but then a year passed, and another, with no sign of change in the lump or indication that it was causing any problems.

I did not give Robert's health much thought, though, until others began to mention it with increasing frequency in the years after he retired as poet laureate. Nancy offered Robert a ride home after one of the Poetry Hoots, and he accepted. This was a first. She told me later that he was breathing so hard, she wasn't sure he would make it to the car. She asked him if he wanted her to take him to the hospital. He said that would not be necessary.

"What do you think we should do?" Nancy said when she reported the incident. "There's clearly something wrong. I'll pay for a doctor's visit. I told him that. I said I'd pay for the emergency room visit. Do you think that's it, the money?"

"I don't know," I said.

"Does he have health insurance?"

"I don't know," I repeated.

"Honestly, I thought he might die right there in my car." Her voice was laced with exasperation and fear.

In the months that followed there was a lot of talk about the situation among the members of the Poet Laureate board, most of whom were women. At times we seemed like a collection of nagging mothers gathered around Robert to poke and prod the odd phenomena of his existence. Something had to be done, the older women insisted. Robert could not go on like this, wheezing and coughing and scaring us half to death, but he did go on like this.

Nancy conferred with members of the Athenaeum board and learned that, in the past year, the Athenaeum had purchased a health insurance plan for Robert. There, too, people were concerned about him. Beyond a five- or ten-dollar co-pay there would be no charge for a doctor's visit, but he refused to go to the doctor.

Robert was not quite as visible around town now that he was no longer poet laureate. I saw him at the monthly Poetry Hoots and when I encountered him by chance on the street. He continued to attend the board meetings, though he was, as he put it, "a recovering poet laureate." We were all surprised that he had any interest in going to the meetings, but he said with some enthusiasm that he would like to be involved. This was another instance that seemed to reveal he needed people more than he let on. When I met up with him now, I was observant, watching for signs of his failing health.

"I'm afraid Robert is going to die," I said to Jim one night.

We were seated at the table eating dinner. Jim glanced up, the fork balanced in his hand, and said, "I'm not sure Robert wants to live." He made this observation calmly, in the tone of one reporting a simple fact.

"He won't go to the doctor. He's got health insurance, but he won't use it."

Jim shrugged. "If he doesn't want to go to the doctor, why should he go to the doctor?"

I was not able to respond with such measured acceptance. "How much longer do you think he can live like this?"

"I don't know. But I don't think Robert believes it really matters whether he lives or dies."

I considered looking at one's own life this way. I could not imagine it.

In the days that followed, I concluded that Jim was right. Robert did not strike me as depressed. It was rather that he looked past the daily hopes and fears that ruled the rest of us. He understood what mattered and what didn't. He had made his peace with the sort of life he had chosen to lead and, by implication, with the death that would follow.

Not long after this, I received a phone call from Nancy, informing me that Robert was in the hospital. He had asked Connie to call an ambulance at one in the morning because he couldn't breathe.

*　*　*

I found him in the elevated hospital bed, propped on pillows, a patterned johnny covering his brittle shoulders. His arms resting on top of the sheet had the spindly look of a sparrow's legs. Seeing his sunken chest beneath the hospital gown made me stop for a moment in the doorway to compose my face. By the time he turned his head, I managed a smile.

He was in the far bed by the window. The other bed, to my relief, was empty. Robert called out hello, his tone spirited, almost jovial.

I sat in a vinyl-covered chair that made a farting sound as I shifted my weight. Copies of the *Portsmouth Herald* and *Foster's Daily Democrat* lay strewn on either side of Robert on the bed. Plastic cups with straws hanging over their edges littered the table, and that hospital smell permeated the air, industrial cleansers barely masking the scent of urine and overcooked macaroni and cheese.

"I take it someone let you know I was here," Robert said.

"Nancy called me."

"Ahh. I'm not sure how she found out."

"She was going to pick you up. For the poetry reading."

"That's right. Oh, dear, I hope she didn't make a trip for nothing."

"She called and Connie told her."

"I'm afraid I gave Mrs. Wilson quite a scare."

"You mean calling the ambulance?"

"Yes. I had to wake her."

"It's a good thing you did."

Robert held my gaze for a moment. The look we exchanged was full of the unspoken. This could be the end, we were admitting, though we would not acknowledge this awful reality with anything more than a lowering of our eyes.

I had come to visit Robert out of a sense of his need, and concern for him. Who would visit him in the hospital? Now, I recognized, I could be counted among his closest friends. There was no one he relied on in any regular way. Along with a few others, I would be all he had, or so I believed at that moment.

It was not until I sat there beside his bed, though, that I felt the full implications of being with him in that stark room. To stare death in the face with someone was a new experience. To do so with a person I knew in ways that now seemed so tentative was beyond anything I could have imagined.

"So how was the reading?" Robert said.

I told him the Poetry Hoot had gone well, and the audience had numbered close to seventy.

"I don't think we ever imagined this when we started, do you? It's been quite a success."

His tone and look were full of pride. I nodded my assent. So this, I saw, was how he was going to play it, by as usual deflecting the attention away from himself and focusing not on his mortality but on what would continue once he was gone.

"What do the doctors say?" I asked in an attempt to shift the conversation back.

"My lungs are not in especially good shape, but they think I may have a chance of getting out of here."

It was then I noticed the paper on the tray table by the bed. "Living will" was written across the top; at the bottom of the sheet,

I saw Robert's signature. This simple one-page form brought home the gravity of the moment in a way that Robert himself, reclining in a hospital bed, did not. I felt both fear and relief—fear at the thought of facing death with him, and relief that someone else was taking care of the details.

"My sister came to visit," he said. "I guess that's an indication of something."

This was the first I had heard of any family connected to Robert. I had somehow never imagined him as having relatives.

A nurse came breezing into the room at that moment. "Mr. Dunn," she called out, "how are we doing?"

"Fine," he said.

She checked the machine that was monitoring his heart rate and left him a menu to fill out for dinner. When she had retreated, her shoes squeaking on the polished floor, I asked how the food was.

"Not bad. It's just that they want me to eat a great deal more than I'm interested in. I've never been much for eating, I'm afraid. They're quite alarmed about my weight."

He gave me a conspiratorial glance, as if to say that I understood the battle in which he was now engaged. The doctors and nurses were inclined to want certain things of him, and though he had no intention of being ungrateful, he was not going to comply with their wishes simply to oblige. Robert seemed to sense, rightly so, that I shared his distrust of institutions and did not like to be told what to do. We both clung to our independence, though he took this a bit further than I ever had. Under the hospital lights, it felt like a new bond between us.

He looked over the dinner options and made a few marks with the pencil the nurse had left. She returned and scooped up the form. When the nurse was gone, I asked, as if the question had just occurred to me, "Where does your sister live?"

"Meredith," he said. "Up by the lakes. The hospital tracked her down, I guess. She was fairly concerned. Concerned enough to drive down here."

I waited, giving him the chance to say more about his sister, but he did not do so. Questions shuffled themselves in my mind. How long would he stay in the hospital, and if he was able to leave, what would come next? Would his sister return? I couldn't voice any of them.

He did not name what was wrong with him, and neither did I. I understood that the label for his condition was a boring topic, at best, and did not ask him about it, though I would learn from others that he was diagnosed with emphysema. They got this information through chance encounters with doctors and nurses when they visited Robert at the hospital. Later I would make a reference to his condition as emphysema, and with a quick, bristling tone, he would correct me. COPD, or Chronic Obstructive Pulmonary Disease, was what he had.

I had come to the hospital without bringing anything, which now seemed terrifically thoughtless, but the standard flowers and cards did not strike me as right for Robert, though he could, it occurred to me now, use something to read. I made this suggestion, and he responded enthusiastically. He gestured toward the television looming down at him from its perch on the wall. "They don't understand why I keep turning that thing off."

I told Robert I would return with some books and made my way to the elevator, aware of a sudden exhaustion that seemed to suck all life from me. It wasn't until I left the room that I understood how draining the effort to appear upbeat had been. I was prepared for this to be one of the last times I might see Robert, though he looked a bit sturdier and more resilient than I had expected. He was, most of all, determinedly cheerful, his sly humor intact. If we had to enter this new territory, he would see that it was not bleak.

* * *

Many emails and phone calls went back and forth during the ten days Robert spent in the hospital. People at the Athenaeum were in touch with Robert's landlady and reported that Connie had declared she couldn't have him back in the house because she was not able to care for a sick person. I received a phone call from Ellie, one of the board members at the Athenaeum who had been instrumental in arranging for the health insurance. Where, she wondered, was Robert going to go? A collective panic set in. None of us knew what to do.

Connie was persuaded, in the end, to take Robert back. The day after his release from the hospital I went to visit. Connie met me at the door and gestured toward the stairs. "You can go on up," she said.

I was curious to see Robert's room, but I felt nervous as I climbed the stairs and knocked timidly on the door.

The door was open a crack. Robert called in a hoarse voice for me to come in. He was seated in an easy chair next to a tray table, in his baggy chinos, a plaid shirt, and a thin, wool bathrobe tied neatly at the waist. His face had the gray, lifeless look I thought it might always have now, but he appeared a bit better than he had in the hospital. The only other pieces of furniture in the room were a straight-backed chair, a single bed, and a couple of open shelves close to the floor. The CD player given to him at the Athenaeum party was perched on one of the shelves with a collection of books. A bare bulb protruded from a socket affixed to the wall over the bed.

I sat in the straight chair and asked Robert how he was doing.

"Well enough, I guess," he said. "They let me out of that place."

I gave him a fresh pile of books I had collected. He gestured toward a stack on the floor and said he had read them all, and I could have them back. I had discovered while he was in the hospital that he went through books at a rapid rate, one or two a day.

The room had the same shrouded feel as the rest of the house. The walls were a sort of putty color, the paint that had been applied decades ago barely clinging to them. Yellowed shades covered two windows, partially obscuring the view of gnarled tree branches and the pond in the distance. A couple of cartons of yogurt were perched on the windowsill, and packets of saltine crackers littered the tray table.

We sat in silence for a few moments, both of us too aware, it seemed, of the intimacy of this meeting. I had first met Robert almost thirteen years ago, here on Whidden Street, and in the time since then, as we were drawn closer in the circle of Portsmouth writers, I had never visited him at his house or gone out to dinner with him or met him in a café for coffee. Although I had observed him, and done so closely, the full nature of his daily life had remained in crucial ways hidden from my prying eyes and those of others. I felt privileged to be given entry to his room but also uncertain of my place here. Robert seemed to accept my visit as one more unlikely situation made necessary by his health.

I was dismayed, but not surprised, by the utterly bare state of the room. It felt far more like a monk's cell than I had imagined it would. The almost complete absence of possessions was breathtaking. I thought of my own house strewn with stuff and felt an uncomfortable prick of self-consciousness. I admired Robert even more after entering his room, but I was alarmed in a way I had not been before. He truly lived on nothing. How was he going to do that now?

I asked if he needed any food. He drew his lips together and shook his head. "No, I have plenty."

Crackers and yogurt did not strike me as plenty, but I saw that determined look on his face. He was drawing a line. He would accept the books and no more.

"The visiting nurse came to see me yesterday," he said. He seemed to offer this as proof that he was being taken care of and had no need of further assistance. "She was rather taken aback to discover there were no outlets in this room. She couldn't plug her laptop in."

"What did she need her laptop for?"

"Apparently she uses it to take notes." He smiled in a way that indicated he relished defeating the expectations of the nurse and the requirements of her portable technology.

"Does she think you're going to be able to manage?"

"She doesn't want me climbing the stairs too much, for a few days at least. She says I need to rest."

This sounded ominous to me, but Robert offered it with a breezy nonchalance. He did not seem to be worried about being confined to his room.

"Can you see the buffleheads from your window?" I asked, referring to the ducks that took up residence on the pond in winter. "They're still here."

"I noticed they hadn't left yet."

"They were doing a funny little dance the other day, sort of running at each other on top of the water."

"I expect they're feeling their oats. It *is* spring after all." After a pause, he reached for a newspaper clipping on the tray table and handed it to me. "I thought you might enjoy this."

A blurry shot of a bride and groom and a headline with their names gazed up at me in black and white. At the bottom, in Robert's hand, was the notation "Downeast Coastal Press, 17 August 1999." The rather large bride and equally large groom appeared to be well into their fifties, suggesting a second marriage. I scanned the copy quickly. It was a typical small-town announcement that included a description of the bride's polyester satin gown with "a scalloped neckline, princess seams, and flattering Basque waist." The three-layer cake had been made by the sister of the groom and cut by the aunt of the bride. The details were poignant and sweet, reflective of a world wonderfully removed from the surface sophistication of a place like New York. The clipping was a piece of Americana, but I wasn't sure why Robert wanted me to see it. The announcement seemed innocuous enough. I thought there must be some subtle detail I was missing.

"It sounds like a real Maine wedding," I said.

"Yes, it's quite wonderful, isn't it? I found it lying about and thought of you."

"It's very funny." I added this, though I was not sure I had picked up on what he intended and felt that laughing at this unknown bride and groom might be unkind.

When I took my leave a few minutes later, I promised to return. I told him to have Connie call if he needed anything. Shortly after this visit, I received the following letter from Robert, on heavy paper in his beautiful penmanship, the letters carefully formed by the ink of a fountain pen:

Portsmouth, NH
March 9, 2004

Dear Katie,

The visiting nurse tells me that I'm still alive. I had thought as much, but it's nice to have it all official. And life does seem less daunting after a full night's sleep without anyone coming around to stick a needle into you. Anyway, much thanks for your help and moral support. It made the world seem much more possible. Unlikely as always, but possible.

Cheers,
Robert

Included with the letter was a Xerox copy of the clipping from the *Downeast Coastal Press.*

* * *

We all expected that Robert might slip away in his room on the second floor of Connie's house, but he gradually returned to his regular routine. A few weeks after his hospitalization, he began going in to the Athenaeum for an hour or two. I saw him again in the afternoons if I drove into town. He walked slowly, head lowered, and stopped to sit on the wall by the old cemetery. I saw him there a few times, his shoulders hunched together as though folding his body inward. The cemetery was only a block from Whidden Street, and his resting there was an indication of just how much effort the walk into town took. But other than his slowed gait and rest stops, he appeared unchanged. He wore the same trench coat and tweed cap and clutched the same coffee cup. The cigarette, though, was absent, and a rumor went around town among the writers and others who stopped me to ask about Robert that he had quit smoking. We traded this news with a sort of wonder, as if discussing someone who had come back from the dead.

Over dinner one night, I said to Jim, "Robert chose life."

Jim nodded.

"I didn't think he would. But he called that ambulance. And now look at him."

"I guess he wanted to live after all."

I felt a personal vindication that Robert had pulled through this crisis, as if I had somehow willed him to live.

9.

Tea Ceremony

On a blustery day, with a fine rain spitting into the wind, I found Robert standing at the head of Whidden Street in his trench coat and hat. His body curved in a question mark, he seemed to be leaning on the air, his gaze, as usual, fixed on an inscrutable distance. If he had been waiting long, or worried that I might not show up, he did not betray it, though I was a few minutes late.

I had been at my desk upstairs working on the next novel. Mornings are the time when I work best, but I'm not an early riser, by New Hampshire standards at least. Everyone in the state claims to get up at four or five in the morning. When I first moved here, I thought of it as some sort of collective insanity. My appointment to meet Robert was for one o'clock, that hour when a last burst of writing often overtakes me. I closed the file minutes before one, shut down the computer, and tried to shake off the annoyance I felt.

I had been anticipating, with some anxiety, driving down Whidden Street and having to back up the length of the street to get out. This was a challenging maneuver I had dreaded, and never really perfected, when I lived there. I was relieved, then, to discover Robert waiting at the head of the street. He ambled slowly toward the car when I pulled over. As he climbed into the front seat, I saw that he was wearing a pair of white boat sneakers beneath his corduroy pants. They were so out of character, I had to look away.

"Thanks for waiting there," I said.

"I thought I'd save you trying to get in and out."

He managed, with some effort, to close the car door, and I drove on. "So how are you doing?" I asked.

"Much better." The tone in his voice was full of the spirit I remembered. He truly did seem stronger. "I'm back at work."

"You're doing all right walking there?" I asked.

"Oh, yes. The visiting nurse said the exercise is good for me."

"They must be glad to have you back at the Athenaeum."

He gave me that wry smile. "They made quite a fuss over me."

Robert asked about the latest poetry reading and what was going on with the current laureate's project. It was a pattern I would come to know well, Robert quickly shifting the talk away from questions about his health.

I drove out of town to an office park near the highway. He directed me to a suite at the back of the complex. I saw the sign affixed to the door as I pulled into the parking space: Portsmouth Regional Hospital, Second Wind Pulmonary Rehabilitation. He grimaced when I told him to have fun. "I'm not sure that's the word for it," he said as he stepped from the car.

When I returned to get him an hour later, he was waiting out at the curb. In this and other small ways, he tried to cause the least amount of trouble for those of us who drove him to his appointments. He did not speak as he settled himself into the seat. His breathing was slow and labored. I listened to the raspy passage of air in and out of his lungs and wondered if putting him through rehab was a good idea, but after a moment he breathed more easily.

I waited until we were out of the office park to speak. "So how did it go?" I said.

The words felt strange, the sort of conversation I was more used to having with my husband than Robert. My conversations with Robert had almost always been about books, or poetry readings, or our writing. I did not want to make small talk with him. It seemed a sort of desecration, yet it didn't feel right to sit in silence, either.

"All right, I guess. The physical therapist seemed to think there was some hope for me."

"What do they have you doing?"

"I have to breathe into a little thing and make a ball go up and down." He said this in a rueful tone, the ridiculousness of it obvious, though he would admit to the necessity of this foolishness. "I spent a little time on the treadmill. Apparently I've got some lung capacity. And with practice, I can get more."

"That's wonderful." I hadn't thought anything more than maintaining his current functioning would be possible, but here we were talking about improvement, about Robert getting better. This was the first in a long series of moments that would have the feel of the miraculous.

Robert did not, in this period of recovery, ask for help, though he reluctantly accepted it. Various members of the Poet Laureate board made it their business to find out what he needed and conveyed requests to the rest of us by email. We quickly learned that we had to make our offers of assistance as delicately as possible. Robert recoiled from any hints of charity and only took help when it was absolutely necessary, when he could not find a way around involving others.

I drove him to and from his rehab appointments a few times that spring. There were plenty of other appointments, I learned, he did not tell me about. Instead he took taxis out to the hospital complex and back.

* * *

Now that my book had been published, I drove around New England to give readings at bookstores and libraries where I never knew how many people might show up. Sometimes I might find forty people seated on folding chairs, other times three. I gave the same reading no matter how big or small the crowd, and attempted to answer questions for which I often felt there were no answers. The people who came to these events wanted me to explain the book, something that, like so much of the experience of being published, I had never anticipated. Just because I had written a book did not mean I could explain it; in fact, I seemed to be the last person who could do so. The questions I got at these events made me understand how much the process of writing a novel was a sort of fever dream from which I emerged blinking at the light, not entirely certain what had just happened.

Many readers wanted to know why I created a character as strange as George Tibbits. Like all of my characters, George contains at least a piece of me. I function better than George, and when I'm out in public cheerfully making conversation can sometimes even be mistaken for an extrovert, but his longing to be silent and alone is my longing, too. Beyond that piece of myself I had given him, though, just where did George come from? It wasn't until some time had passed that I thought of Robert and wondered if he was the inspiration for George.

I had not conjured Robert as I was writing the book. He was simply that figure glimpsed below the window on Whidden Street gliding silently toward the center of town. When I went back and retraced the process of writing multiple drafts of the novel, it seemed that George appeared as a character on the page before Robert had arrived as a real character in my life, but since I did not date the handwritten pages that now lie in folders that fill two cardboard boxes, I couldn't be sure. After the fact, however, the two came together in their quiet and seemingly strange ways, although Robert was, in the end, more social than George, a great conversationalist when he chose to be, and in possession of a sharp sense of humor George entirely lacked.

The time I was spending with Robert now, and the questions readers asked about George Tibbits, eddied in my mind, streams sucked into the same pool. To what extent was I more like both of them, Robert and George, than I cared to admit? Were my romantic notions about these two solitary characters completely off base? And did this mean that somehow my understanding of myself was incomplete, clouded, even deluded?

George, the fictional character, and Robert, the real character, were mirrors in which I saw my life and my choices reflected. I was not, to outward appearances, as solitary as either of them. I had somehow managed to get married and to stay married. I belonged to a world of connections in Portsmouth and farther afield, but in my heart, I often retreated to the solitude these two characters represented. The silent mornings spent writing were the times when I was most myself. These precious, carefully guarded hours were still, after thirteen years of living in Portsmouth and being married, not easily balanced with the rest of what I did. It seemed in these hours when I was absorbed in the writing that George just might be my truest self.

* * *

I was standing in line at the post office when, from behind, someone tapped me on the shoulder. I turned to find Ellie from the Athenaeum board. We exchanged hellos and then she said, "What are we going to do about our friend?"

It took a moment before I realized she was talking about Robert. "He's doing better," I said.

She pursed her lips, as if to say she wasn't sure she agreed with that assessment. "Yes, but he can't stay in that house forever. The stairs are too much for him."

I saw that she was right, but I had avoided thinking about this. I did not want to imagine what might come next for Robert. He seemed, once again, timeless and ageless, as if he could go on living as he always had. One day, I supposed, he would suddenly be gone. Until then, couldn't he keep making his slow, daily walk into town and back?

"Do you think he would consider applying for disability?" she said. "You know he's not sixty-five yet, so he doesn't qualify for senior housing. But if we got him on disability, he'd qualify."

The revelation that Robert was not yet sixty-five was surprising. I considered her suggestion and imagined Robert bristling at it. He might reject this sort of help as interference. Still, it was worth a try. "I don't know if he'd agree," I said. "But I'd talk to him about it. He might go for it."

"Are you saying you would talk to him, or do you want me to?"

"I think it'd be better if you did." I could not quite imagine such a conversation.

Ellie nodded, a look of conviction and relief on her face, and said she would attempt it.

A few weeks later, when I ran into Ellie at the supermarket, she said, "I have good news. Our friend has agreed. We're going ahead with the disability application. He says he'll be happy to move to the public housing."

I felt like I had been roped into a clandestine plot as I leaned over my shopping cart in the pasta aisle discussing the dilemma of Robert. How much help would he accept? And how much could we

realistically give? I was relieved that Ellie had a plan. I wasn't thinking about how this plan would unfold or what it might mean when
Robert moved. I wanted the situation settled; I wanted to stop wor-
rying about him.

*   *   *

By the summer of 2004, I was no longer giving Robert rides to the rehab appointments. When I asked if he needed help with this, he said he
did not without divulging further information. He may have been finished with the rehab, or he may have decided he preferred taking taxis.
I didn't know. He blended back into the landscape that fall and winter.
The crisis was past, and he no longer needed, or wanted, assistance.

One afternoon at the Pic 'n Pay, I exited my car to find Connie
getting out of a car parked nearby. She was walking with a cane now,
but in every other way she looked just as she had when we lived on
Whidden Street. Her blouse was tucked carefully into a faded blue
skirt, and her swollen legs were covered in thick stockings of a vaguely orange hue. A young woman came around to the side of the car to
help her make the walk into the store.

I said hello, and Connie raised her head. Her eyes had a thin,
clouded look.

"Oh, hello," she said. "Have you seen Robert recently? He's doing
quite well."

"Yes. I'm so glad he's back at work."

"You should come visit him. He gets lonely, you know."

I smiled in uneasy acknowledgment of this statement, said it
was good to see her, and went on to my shopping. Robert? Lonely?
He was not looking for me to visit him. Perhaps Connie was lonely
and would like visitors, but not Robert. Still, she had planted the
seed, and I would remember her words.

Maybe she was right, and Robert, for all his iconoclastic ways, was lonely. I thought of all the times people had asked me didn't I find it lonely to go off on writing retreats or sit at my desk by myself each morning? I had always bristled at these questions. In a culture where being an outsized extrovert is the admired norm, how do you explain that you like spending time alone? With Connie's comment echoing in my mind, however, I began to wonder about the solitude Robert had embraced and my own desire for it. If forced to, I would admit that writing was lonely sometimes, but mostly I denied this. If I let those feelings of loneliness in, if I went running back to the world of human interaction, I would never finish the work that mattered so much to me.

The poet Marianne Moore claimed that "the cure for loneliness is solitude." I had always imagined I understood the difference between the two. I had cultivated the ability to spend time in solitude out of preference, necessity, and plain stubbornness. Now I found myself wondering how distinct the two states really were, how often I might have clung to a solitude that quickly devolved into loneliness.

I had believed, since those first years of seeing Robert around town, that he did not suffer from the conflicts I did. He navigated the back and forth between solitude and the world of people with a steely-eyed clarity. Connie's remark suggested we might be more alike than I had thought, both of us driven in our silent ways, both of us experiencing those times of loneliness we didn't want to own.

* * *

Ellie kept me updated on the progress of the disability application. It was complicated and went slowly, but almost a year after our first conversation she reported that the application was successful. Later Robert would comment that the disability checks added up to the most money he had ever had in his life. In June of 2005 he was assigned a place in the Feaster Apartments and began making plans to move. Just a couple of blocks from Congress Street and Market Square, the six-story building provides housing for senior citizens and the disabled. I had passed it countless times without paying much attention to the structure, beyond noting that it was a rather ugly modern eyesore next to the historic houses farther down the block.

I was out of town when Robert moved, but I received email updates from members of the Poet Laureate board who had helped him. In July, I sent Robert an invitation for the launch party for my second novel and received the following response. Our new independent bookstore, RiverRun, was hosting the event in a dance club on the third floor of a brick building downtown. I had noted that an elevator was available when I sent the invitation.

Portsmouth, NH
July 2, 2005

Dear Katie,

Thanks for the tip. I'll hope to take the elevator on July 12, bringing Charles Williams* if I can but remember.

I did get a telephone. It felt a bit like adopting a pet rattlesnake. Although it's possible—even likely—that rattlesnakes are unjustly maligned. They may keep the mice down, you know, and tourists. Anyway it answers to 431-6960. Or at least I think it does . . .

Cheers,
Robert

* He is referring to a book by Charles Williams, the British novelist and theologian, that Jim had expressed interest in.

I was not able to speak with Robert for more than a couple of minutes at the launch party, but I called him a few days later. He asked about my travels with the book and commented that it was a good kickoff. I told him where I would be going on my book tour. The conversation went on like this, back and forth, until I realized that I was chatting with him as though he were one of my sisters. This felt so strange that I almost forgot to ask if I could come visit, the purpose of the call.

The short walk from the street to the main entrance of the Feaster Apartments is bordered by flower beds and a couple of benches. On the afternoon I went to see Robert, the benches were full. An elderly, overweight woman wearing a worn housedress and slippers sat smoking a cigarette with a Chihuahua on her lap. A man leaned on a walker, his oxygen canister in a wheeled container beside him, tubes running over his ears into his nostrils. A younger man with bushy hair and eyebrows stood near one of the benches with his head thrust toward the sun. I recognized him as one of the regulars at the Salvation Army soup kitchen where I sometimes volunteered. He never spoke beyond a mumbled thank-you when I handed him a plate of food. I had assumed that he was mentally ill and possibly homeless and was relieved to discover that he lived here. None of the residents taking the air gave any indication of being aware of each other or of me.

I rang the buzzer inside and, after a moment, heard Robert's raspy "Hello?" through the intercom. He buzzed me into the lobby, where a couple more women were seated on a vinyl-covered couch that looked like it could have been taken from the booth of an old diner. "Hello, doll," one of them said as she gave me a big, toothless smile. "Pretty day, huh?"

"Beautiful," I said.

"You moving in?" She inclined her head toward the cardboard box I carried.

"No. Just taking some things to a friend."

"That's nice." She turned her head to follow my progress down the dimly lit hall with its yellowed linoleum. I half-expected her to follow me.

A man rounded the corner with a cocker spaniel on a leash. He appeared to be a good deal younger than any of the other residents, but he walked with a decided limp. He nodded at me and made his way calmly past a large sign fixed to the wall that read, NO DOGS ALLOWED IN BUILDING. Out in the lobby, I heard him call out, "Good afternoon, ladies."

Robert was waiting with the door to his apartment ajar, his face just visible around the edge of the frame. We might have been actors in a play, both of us given roles we could not have imagined assuming before. Robert having his own place and welcoming me as his guest were altogether strange and new.

He ushered me inside and, when I asked where I should put the box, made a vague wave of his hand. "Oh, anywhere."

The room was dark, lit only by a single, uncurtained window with a view of a driveway and the wall of the building next door. When my eyes had adjusted to the grayness, I saw that there was almost no furniture, other than two easy chairs with a coffee table between them, and a small bookcase pushed against one wall. I set the box on the floor.

I had brought Robert a collection of mugs and salad plates salvaged from the yard sale boxes in my basement. The plates, from the 1940s or '50s, were bright yellow with bouquets of flowers at the edges and had a distinctly vintage look. My sister had picked them up in a thrift shop in Ann Arbor years earlier and passed them on to me in one of her many moves. I had added to these items a set of salt and pepper shakers in the shape of watering cans, also with a vintage look, that came from the collection that was threatening to take over my kitchen and the rest of the house. For good measure, I had included a trivet and a poster of a Matisse painting that was only slightly frayed around the edges. When I had reviewed these offerings in my own house, they struck me as a fine assortment of treasures, but here in Robert's empty apartment, they seemed like paltry cast-offs. I should have considered what he truly needed—furniture and rugs—though it was hard to imagine him possessing such things.

"I brought you some stuff," I said. "I don't know if you need any dishes . . ."

Robert peered down into the box. "Certainly. I can use dishes."

A glance toward the little galley kitchen at one side of the room revealed open shelves with a set of matching dinner plates and cups and saucers. I wondered where these had come from. My plates were a motley, chipped bunch, but maybe he could use them for small servings, which was all Robert consumed anyway.

I unfurled the Matisse poster. "I thought you could use something for your walls."

Robert regarded the image of a woman reclining on a sofa with a cool eye. "Ah, Matisse," he said in that completely unreadable way of his.

He didn't like it, I told myself, and would not hang it on his wall. I was right. The poster disappeared after my visit, never to be seen again.

We both stood by the box a moment longer, until Robert gestured toward one of the two chairs. It was covered in dirty green upholstery; some areas were nearly bare of any covering or disgorged ragged puffs of stuffing. Robert took the chair across from me, which was just as worn, and asked if I would like some tea, or maybe wine? He had some chilled white wine in the refrigerator. He was revealing himself, once again, to be far more resourceful than I had given him credit for being. I said that tea would be fine, despite the heat of the day, though the darkened apartment felt much cooler than the outdoors.

Robert went to the little nook that formed his kitchen and put the water on to boil. He was in a decidedly cheerful mood, far happier than I had expected to find him. It was clear, as he assembled the teacups and a plate of cookies on a tray, and set it on the table between our chairs, that he was delighted with everything about this—being the host, and offering me something to eat and drink, and having a place he could call his own. I had thought the transition to the apartment would be difficult, but just the opposite appeared to be the case.

I watched as Robert poured some of the hot water from the kettle into a squat white teapot. He swirled the water around and dumped it into the sink. He proceeded to take a box of loose tea from the cupboard and spoon some into the teapot, then to add more water from the kettle. All of this was done with the precision of a Japanese master at a tea ceremony, as if it were a ritual he had performed many times before. When he brought the teapot to the table between our chairs, he let it sit a few minutes before placing a small silver strainer over my china cup and pouring. On the tray beside the plate of butter cookies sat a pitcher of milk and a sugar bowl. He gestured toward them. "Do you take milk or sugar in your tea?" he asked.

"Neither," I said.

"Neither do I."

This seemed, for the moment, a significant coincidence.

"I'm quite comfortable, as you can see," he said, inclining his head in the direction of the compact kitchen. "And I can walk downtown easily from here."

"How are your neighbors?" I asked.

"Oh, they've been very welcoming. Some of them are quite mad, but then I'm rather mad myself."

"Do you know the psychologist Albert Ellis?"

"Yes, he's been around forever, hasn't he?"

"*The New Yorker* did a piece on his ninetieth birthday a while back. He says, 'All humans are out of their fucking minds.'"

Convulsed with laughter, Robert leaned forward, his shoulders shaking. I laughed with him, but within seconds, he was overcome by racking coughs and gasping for breath. I made a mental note to avoid making him laugh like this in the future.

When Robert had regained his breath, I said, "I saw that tall man out front, the one with the bushy hair. I've seen him at the soup kitchen, at the Salvation Army."

"Ethan. He's always out front or over in Market Square."

"And the guy with the dog. Does he live here? The sign said, 'No dogs allowed.'"

"That's Pete. He's one of the saner ones. He plants all the flowers around the building and takes care of them. They overlook the dog. It's not too big."

"What about that woman with the shopping cart downtown? Does she live here?"

"Ah, yes, Charlotte. She's quite a character. She lives in Kittery actually. She goes back and forth across the bridge with that cart."

I had met Charlotte at the soup kitchen as well. She always arrived early and helped us set the tables. One time she came with a bouquet of carnations that she distributed to all the diners because it was her birthday. It made sense that Robert knew the street people of Portsmouth. He was, in a way, one of them.

"So you're managing meals all right?" I asked.

Robert shot me one of his looks, as if to say I had no business inquiring about something as personal as his diet. "I'm afraid I have too much food. People keep bringing me more. I have plenty in the freezer, and I can heat it up in the microwave."

I had not noticed the shiny white appliance on the kitchen counter. "Where did you get the microwave?"

"My friend Lynne bought it for me."

I waited for further explanation. Who was this friend Lynne? I thought I knew all Robert's friends, the circle of writers connected through the Poet Laureate Program. This assumption, like so many others I had made in the past about Robert and would make in the future, was incorrect.

When he offered nothing more about the mysterious Lynne, I said, "That's very useful, a microwave."

"Yes, so I've discovered." He brought his hands together the way he often did, fingertips pointed toward the ceiling, reminding me of the old game we used to play when I was a child, "Here's the church, here's the steeple." He seemed to indicate, with this gesture, that the matter of his physical well-being was closed to further discussion. The microwave gleaming on the counter sat there as irrefutable proof that my prying questions were unnecessary.

* * *

A few days later, I was preparing a salad for dinner when the phone rang. I propped the phone against my ear, continued to shred lettuce, and said hello.

A soft and raspy voice responded, "Oh, hello, Katie. It's Robert."

"Robert," I said, trying to hide my surprise. Though I had called him, I had somehow not imagined he could, or would, call me. "How are you doing?"

"Quite well, but I have a favor to ask of you. I was wondering if you could drive me to the Rite Aid. There's a table I saw there that would do nicely for a desk."

"Sure, I can give you a ride."

"There's no rush, of course. Whenever you have the time. I wouldn't ask, but it's just that I can't bring the table back on the senior citizen van."

"I've got my station wagon. It will fit in that, right?"

"Yes, that's what I was thinking."

We arranged that I would pick him up the following afternoon at three. He was waiting on the bench outside his building when I pulled in. At Rite Aid, Robert went straight to a display of folding tables near the front of the store.

"I can get that," I said.

"Oh, I can handle this," he responded.

The table cost twenty dollars and was not much more than heavy cardboard attached to a couple of metal tubes for legs. Long and skinny, it was the size of a conference table. When I set it in the back of the car, I realized that Robert was right, he could handle it. It had the weight of an empty cardboard box.

Back at his apartment, he unfolded the legs and placed the table against the wall by the entrance to the kitchen, then stepped back to admire the arrangement.

"Just right," he said.

He was clearly quite pleased. I smiled. "Now you have a desk."

"Yes, that was really all I needed."

He offered me some wine or tea, but I said I had better be going. He thanked me and ushered me to the door. As I climbed into my car, I thought about how happy Robert seemed in his new place, and how no one would have predicted this turn of events. He was like a teenager allowed to decorate his own room for the first time. Only in the eyes of others could his furniture appear makeshift, the small apartment dark or cramped. To him it was a glorious little kingdom over which he had complete dominion and control.

10.

Next of Kin

The sound of the bells tolling the hour in the North Church steeple was one of the first things that defined the character of Portsmouth for me, and it still does. Even in my half-sleep, as I count the number of rings (*four a.m.*, I tell myself, *go back to sleep*), I am listening to the past. And then a minute later, another bell sounds from the cupola of the old Quaker Meeting House, nearby in the South End. The two clocks, never in sync, measure the silence as much as interrupt it. They are voices arguing for a different kind of time, slower and less fractured than what we know now.

At night the lit steeple of the church shines above the treetops, a white beacon. Like the reflective surface of the pond rippling in the dark, the sight of the steeple and the sound of its bells make me stop what I am doing for a moment to look up from the page I am reading or the pot I am scrubbing at the sink. The summer when Robert moved into his apartment the steeple was not illuminated, though, and the view from the kitchen window felt oddly empty. In mid-July, the top of the steeple had been removed and scaffolding placed around the base. The badly decayed structure was under renovation by carpenters who would use hand tools similar to those used in the construction of the original steeple in 1855. When I stood at the sink after dinner, I found myself searching for the missing landmark.

I was away off and on over the summer, but I called Robert and went to see him a few times. Seated facing me in his apartment, he could not suddenly end our exchange and walk away as he had in the past. As abrupt and confounding as our conversations had sometimes been, they had not left me wanting more. For everything Robert withheld, he gave in equal measure. His wry observations, quick wit, and agile mind made up for what was missing of a personal nature. With someone else, the lack of a more personal exchange might have felt problematic. With Robert, it had always been oddly charming.

Now that I visited him at his apartment, our friendship was on a different footing. I tried to endure the pauses in our conversations without filling them too quickly, but out of nervousness and lack of patience with his reticence, I went on about my family visits and summer travels, the prevalence of mosquitoes that year, and how my vegetable garden was doing. Robert stuck to books and items in the newspaper. Much of the time what he said was inaudible, causing me to lean halfway out of my chair in an effort to catch the mumbled words. Often I asked him to repeat himself, though this did not necessarily help, even when I made the request twice. After that, I would give up, pretend I had heard him, and nod vaguely. Other times I understood him but was not familiar with the writers he mentioned and again took to responding with an evasive nod. He threw out these literary references without explaining them, as if testing to see what I knew. He seemed in moments to be showing off, though I could hardly blame him. He knew so much.

Books were always the safest and happiest topic. We talked about Henry James's *Portrait of a Lady* and Pat Barker's World War I novels.

How Robert's eyes lit up when we left behind my talk of the weather, and our common acquaintances, and his health. He came fully alive, tapping a deep well of passion, as he recalled a line from a Theodore Roethke poem or conjured a character like James's Isabel Archer, who felt more real (and interesting) than people we actually knew.

Robert repeated the ritual of my first visit by serving tea or wine each time. Sometimes he asked how my work was going, by which he did not mean my freelance writing or teaching. I understood he meant the real work. I was writing my third novel now. Seated in the ragged armchair across from him, I told him about my struggles with repeated drafts. With others, even fellow writers, I tended to give cursory accounts of how the writing was going. "Slowly," I would say, determined to be as vague as possible, unwilling to admit just how frustrating and draining the process could be. By now, it seemed, I should have had the business of writing a novel figured out. I should have known exactly where the book was going, but I didn't.

When Robert asked about my work, I felt that he wanted a real answer, and that he would readily accept and understand whatever I said. Complaints, I knew, he would brush aside, but a true revelation of what it was like to write a novel, how much I threw away and doubted, how many times I started over, was of interest to him. It wasn't so much what he said in response as what he didn't say that I found illuminating and helpful. He did not rush to reassure me that I would finish the book someday, as others did. He did not try to downplay my struggles or give falsely cheerful encouragement. He simply listened and, in doing so, suggested that perhaps this is what I needed to do—sit still and listen for the distant, inner voice.

Time paused as he gave me his quizzical attention. Outside his apartment, life went on at its mad pace, and I dashed from one task to another reviewing the "to do" list in my head, but in that small room everything fell away for the space of an hour. Although I found it difficult to make the time to visit Robert, afterward I was always grateful that I had given up my bike ride or postponed the preparation of dinner. I often reflected on the irony of this; my visits with him, intended to be a help and comfort to him now that he could not get out as much, were really a help and comfort to me.

Robert didn't give in to gossip, overreaction to the latest news, or the common round of handwringing and complaining. This was what much of my conversation with others, even other writers, seemed to consist of, but he stepped past all that nonsense and went to what mattered. I would leave his apartment wishing I had conversations like these more often, ones shaped by the certain knowledge that anything of significance had already been revealed and stood before us at any moment in the most unlikely and ridiculous guise. The pigeon lady. The apple picker.

One day I drove him over to Ceres Bakery. He had mentioned that it was a bit far for him to walk now, but he had a credit there of two hundred dollars, a gift he had received, and he had "barely made a dent" in the sum. I did not ask who had given him the gift, and he did not tell me. As we sat at a small table and one person after another called out hello when they came in for coffee or a sandwich, I thought about how many people in Portsmouth had helped to make Robert's existence possible and how surreptitiously they had done so. It was as if the town was engaged in a great, benevolent conspiracy to help him maintain his independence and privacy, so he could go on writing his poems.

One afternoon shortly after our trip to the bakery, a violent thunderstorm brought down the partially reconstructed North Church steeple and the scaffolding around it. Fortunately, no one was hurt when it landed in the middle of Pleasant Street, just missing pedestrians and cars. Robert told me he had heard a loud bang and thought it must be something other than a thunderclap. The next day, he saw the photo in the newspaper of what was left of the steeple strewn over the street.

* * *

I was lulled in these months into imagining that Robert would go like this indefinitely, happy in his new life in the apartment, but in October Nancy called to say that he was in the hospital again, in intensive care.

I was about to enter his room when a nurse swept up to me. "Are you family?" she said. "Only family members are allowed in intensive care."

I was not his daughter, and clearly not his sister. Cousin wasn't right, either. The pause while I attempted to compose an answer went on too long. Finally I said, "I'm his niece."

I was aware as I spoke of a complete lack of conviction in my voice. I made the words sound more like a question than a statement of fact. The nurse stared at me for a moment, jaw clenched, as though deciding whether to accept my fabrication or not, before she walked into the room, in that authoritative way nurses have, and said, "Mr. Dunn, your niece is here to see you."

Robert was breathing into a tube that was attached to a machine making a great deal of noise. He gazed at me over the plastic mouthpiece and nodded. All right, then, his eyes said, you'll be my niece now.

I sat by the bed and smiled at him, as it was impossible for him to talk. His face was drawn in the concentrated effort of getting air in and out of his lungs.

When the breathing treatment was over, the machine unhooked, he sank back on the pillow and asked me what was new in the world out there, gesturing with his hand toward the window. I made some stock answer before asking, "Does your sister know you're here?"

He gave me a startled look, and I understood that I had breached an unspoken agreement by mentioning her. It was the first time either of us had referred to her since his last hospitalization. "No, I don't think she does."

"Don't you think she should be notified?"

"I suppose so. She's not well herself, you know."

Robert found a scrap of paper in the pile of stuff on the tray by his bed and wrote his sister's phone number on it. He passed the paper to me grudgingly, as though informing me I had broken a rule. His family was not to be involved in this. He lay back on the bed stiffly.

I babbled on inanely about the fall foliage, and our cat Zane, now elderly and sick with cancer, and a trip I had taken the previous week on a freelance assignment. Robert accepted my ragbag of news with a rigid reserve. I heard myself attempting to fill the space between us with a wall of talk and wanted to stop, but I couldn't. The less he said, the more I felt compelled to rush in with any words I could grab. The sight of him lying there, strain etched in every line of his body, elicited a manic, noisy response from me. His silence scared me now.

When the nurse arrived with food arranged in little mounds on a sectioned tray, I said good-bye. I drove home in a numb state of dread. Robert was not going to drift out of this world in his sleep one night. The end was going to be painful for both of us, though I was focused, at that moment, on my own pain. I did not want to be present at this slow-motion free fall.

* * *

I sent an email around to the Poet Laureate board members and other writers in town to let them know Robert was in intensive care. The looks on the faces of the nurses, the term "intensive care," the number of machines that now surrounded Robert's bed—all of it signaled a ratcheting of the stakes. The earlier crises seemed like mere blips that had been easily surmounted. This was different.

I dialed the number Robert had given me for his sister. After several rings, a woman said hello. Her voice was low and hoarse. I explained who I was and why I was calling.

"I guess you call him Robert," she said. "We call him Bob."

I waited for her to say more, but there was nothing but a long, raspy silence on the other end. I could not imagine calling Robert by the diminutive Bob, which seemed too informal and undignified.

"I was afraid of this when he moved into that apartment, that he'd end up back in the hospital," she finally said. Her reference to the apartment seemed to indicate that she had been there, which was news to me. "I don't know if I can get down there. I'll see. Thank you for letting me know."

With this the conversation ended.

I could not imagine a time that would come after these days in the hospital for Robert. His sister may not have felt any urgency, but I did. The situation called for action. This was how I responded to what was most difficult or perplexing. I did *something*, whether this involved simply making a phone call, or sending a card, or cooking a casserole dish for a friend in need. I executed some act, large or small, that made me feel I was taking charge; I managed my anxiety and fear by staying busy. I discovered now, however, that there was nothing to be done, and I fell into a sort of paralysis, a dumb sense that I remained in a constant state of waiting.

* * *

I heard the buoyant notes of women's voices as I approached Robert's room. His condition had been upgraded, and he was no longer in intensive care. I found Mimi and one of the nurses engaged in happy chatter, the nurse waiting to take a thermometer from Robert's mouth, Mimi seated in a chair at the foot of the bed. A fellow writer and the new poet laureate in Portsmouth, Mimi was one of the first friends I had made when we moved to New Hampshire. We had conferred often about Robert's situation over the past year and usually tried to time our visits so we didn't overlap.

While Robert gazed blankly over the thermometer, the nurse and Mimi exchanged updates on their children, who had attended high school together. The nurse removed the thermometer and announced that he was not running a fever. "See?" Mimi said. "You're normal, Robert."

He smiled weakly.

"They'll be sending you home any day now, right?"

He shrugged as if to say he did not share her certainty or enthusiasm.

"He's doing much better," the nurse said.

"I can tell. You've got color in your cheeks, Robert."

He shrugged again, clearly unimpressed with this development.

"Robert was the Poet Laureate of Portsmouth, you know," Mimi said to the nurse.

"Really?" the nurse responded in a surprised tone.

"He can still claim the title. It's a position you hold for life."

"Like being president?" I said.

"I rather think not," Robert said.

"He was the second poet laureate," Mimi informed the nurse. "He set the standard for the rest of us."

Robert's eyebrows shot up, an instantaneous expression of his disdain for hyperbole of any sort. "I don't know about that," he said.

"Oh, yes, you did. A very high one, as a matter of fact." Mimi beamed at him, and Robert dipped his head, grudgingly accepting the praise.

The nurse jotted something in the chart and placed it in the holder at the foot of the bed. She told Mimi how nice it was to have seen her and left. Once she was gone, Mimi produced the latest copy of *Poetry* magazine from a bag at her feet and set it on the tray table by the bed.

"Ah, thank you," Robert said. "I haven't read that issue yet."

"There's some good stuff in it. Bad stuff, too."

"As always."

"Yes, as always."

Mimi had a way of making the room seem full, and the situation ordinary, that I could not pull off. I appreciated the ease of her joking with Robert and the nurse. For a moment, my dread lifted.

Robert appeared tired and unable to sustain much conversation. Mimi and I discussed the latest poetry reading while he lay propped on a pillow, content, it seemed, to let us do the talking. We took our leave before long.

On the way out, I told Mimi about the nurse who had questioned my status as a family member on my first visit. "How ridiculous," she snapped. "Robert doesn't have any family. We're his family."

On subsequent visits, I noticed that the nurses seemed a bit more solicitous and less rushed as they went in and out. They no longer gave me probing looks, as if trying to determine what motivated me to take on a charity case like Robert. I attributed the change to Mimi's magic. Perhaps it was her connection with the nurse who was on duty that day, or her mention of Robert's position as poet laureate, or maybe it was simply the fact that Robert had visitors who appeared to be solidly middle class, their presence suggesting he could not be consigned to the merely indigent, that made the nurses treat me, and Robert, with greater deference. I was never asked about my relationship with Robert again, though there would be other times when he landed in intensive care.

* * *

I felt the change as soon as I entered the room. The place seemed to have become more light and airy, without the sound of the breathing machine or a curtain partially drawn around the bed. Robert was seated in a chair, and he greeted me with a smile and a confident calm.

The bed was covered in newspapers—*The Boston Globe*, *The New York Times*, and an assortment of local papers. I nodded toward them. "I see you're keeping informed."

"Dick brings them to me. The man who works at the library."

Richard, a local historian and research associate in the library's Special Collections, was an older man I often saw bustling in and out of the post office or seated in the periodicals section at the library reading the paper. I had not known, until now, that he had any connection to Robert.

"He brings the papers every day?" I asked.

"Yes. He's quite regular in his rounds."

I glanced at the headlines. "Two thousand dead. For what?"

"How astonishing to discover there were no weapons of mass destruction in Iraq."

"We knew that, didn't we?"

Robert nodded in assent.

"So how did all those bozos in Washington not know?"

"I don't think they cared."

In the years when I first knew Robert, we had never discussed national news or politics. This changed when I began driving him to and from his rehab appointments, and I searched for some topic to fill the gaps of silence. I discovered that Robert followed the news closely and was passionate about the folly of the war in Iraq.

"Do you have enough to read besides newspapers?" I asked.

He pointed to a collection of books on the table by the bed. "Plenty. People keep bringing me books."

I spotted David Sedaris's latest book in the stack and asked him how he liked it.

"He's wonderful, but he makes me laugh so hard it sets off the heart monitor and the nurses come running." He had that impish look on his face that said he wouldn't deliberately make any trouble, but if his laughter caused a commotion, it was a small victory for humanity in this sterile place.

We talked about some of the other books he had been reading, and then, when I was about to leave, he said, as if it had just occurred to him, "I've given them permission to talk with you, by the way."

I couldn't think for a moment what he meant. "The doctors?"

"Yes. And the social worker."

I waited for more, but he said nothing. There was no question of my agreeing to this arrangement. It had been done.

The light was flashing on the answering machine when I arrived home that afternoon. The message was from a social worker at the hospital. Could I give her a call? There were some things she wanted to discuss with me.

"He wants to go home," she told me when I reached her.

"Do you think he can manage?"

"We're worried about his meals. I'm trying to get him set up with Meals on Wheels. They'll bring one meal a day. He's agreed to that."

She explained that the visiting nurse would come for at least the first few weeks. If all this was in place, she thought he would be all right. I said I would check on him regularly and that there were others who could do errands for him and bring him food if he needed it, though even as I spoke these words, I wondered how much help we could realistically provide.

I was not, I was certain, suited to this role for which Robert had appointed me, yet in an odd way I felt honored to have been chosen by him. My reaction, like so much of what would follow, was full of ambivalence and confusion, dread and anxious hope, pride and denial. Later it occurred to me that I had claimed to be his niece that day in the hospital. Now he had simply made my status as a near relative official. But why did he give my name to the social worker? There were other candidates who were more likely choices, at least in terms of being caretakers. I was not exactly the motherly, soup-making sort. No doubt this is why he chose me. He didn't want someone who would hover over him.

* * *

The next time I went to visit, I found an elderly couple seated in chairs on either side of Robert's bed. The man wore a tweed jacket and tie, the woman a calf-length skirt and sweater that fell over her small frame like drapery. I stood awkwardly at the foot of the bed, a shopping bag full of books in hand, while Robert introduced us.

The couple gave me questioning glances, as though they could not imagine who I was. I examined them in a similar fashion.

"It's good to see you looking so well," the woman said.

"Yes," the man added, with no conviction whatsoever.

"We don't want to tire you," the woman said.

"No," the man echoed.

Robert nodded, the only gesture he seemed capable of making. "It's good of you to come."

"We wanted to," the woman said vaguely.

"Yes," the man said.

"You take care of yourself." The woman rose unsteadily to her feet. "Everyone has been asking after you."

"They have," the man added.

With that they said good-bye, maneuvered around me, and made their way slowly out of the room.

I met Robert's gaze and waited for him to speak when they had disappeared down the hall. "I know them from the Athenaeum," he said. He did not provide any further information.

I was beginning to piece together an ill-defined picture of the large number of people who knew Robert and cared about him. It was clear from the looks the older couple had given me, and I had returned, that Robert had managed to convince each of us we were his only close friends. I had misjudged how carefully he orchestrated his life, parceling out requests for help among a wider circle of friends than I had imagined. This struck me as another example of Robert's calculation and cleverness, though it came with a certain sadness. How much he had done to guard his privacy and maintain the appearance of independence.

Robert's voice was still raspy, but his eyes were brighter. "I have good news," he said. "They're planning to send me home tomorrow. That is, if nothing unforeseen happens overnight."

"That's wonderful," I responded, aware that my tone was not particularly genuine. I could only think about what this next step would mean. "You probably don't want all these books then."

"No. I'm afraid I've accumulated quite a bit of stuff." He gestured toward a potted plant on the windowsill and piles of newspapers and magazines beside it. "I'm not sure what I'm going to do with all of it."

"Do you need a ride?"

"Well, yes, that would be nice."

If I hadn't made the offer, I suspected that he would have taken a cab.

The next morning, Robert was seated in the chair, dressed and waiting for me, a plastic bag full of books and magazines at his feet.

I asked him if he wanted to take the plant, and he shook his head. I never learned who had brought that bit of cheer. A nurse arrived with a wheelchair and accompanied us downstairs. She waited while I retrieved the car from the parking lot and, when I pulled up, helped Robert into the front seat. The day was gray and chilly.

"Where's your coat?" I asked as we drove away.

"I'm afraid I left home a little quickly and didn't have time to get it."

"When the ambulance came?"

"Yes. It takes them about thirty seconds."

"That's an advantage of your location." His apartment building was next door to the fire station.

"Well, yes, and a disadvantage."

The day before, reclining in the hospital bed, Robert had truly looked better. He was more spirited, quicker to speak, and exuded a bit of his old steadiness. He had seemed, if not in command of his situation at that moment, ready to take command once again, but in the car he appeared shrunken and barely able to breathe, let alone talk. He managed one long, rasping breath after another, his small chest heaving. I feared they were sending him home too soon, that his determination to return to the apartment was not just foolish but dangerous.

I waited to speak again until I had navigated the twisting road away from the hospital and made the turn onto Middle Road. "Do you need anything?" I asked. "Food or anything? We could stop and I could go in."

"I have some prescriptions I need to pick up. The doctor called them in."

I glanced over at him. I could see he didn't have breath to say more. His face was pulled tight in exhaustion. "Do you want me to take you to the apartment and then go pick them up?"

He nodded and choked out a relieved, "Yes." After a minute, he added, "I need to take one of the medications in an hour."

"How about some food? What do you need?"

He took a wheezy breath before responding. "I don't need anything. I have plenty at the apartment."

I knew what "plenty" meant in Robert's case, but I wasn't going to argue with him. Getting him home seemed all that mattered at the moment.

When we reached his building, he insisted that I did not need to walk him inside. I watched as he climbed out of the car and made his way laboriously to the front door, the plastic bag thumping against his side. I resisted the urge to jump out of the car and go after him.

A small crowd milled around the window at the pharmacy. I unzipped my jacket, too hot in the close, overheated space. The pharmacist on duty was an older man I recognized from my own trips to the drugstore. I told him I was there to pick up Robert's prescriptions, and he hunted through the little wire baskets. "I don't have anything under that name," he said.

"The doctor called the order in from the hospital," I said. "This morning."

The pharmacist stiffened and told me to wait a moment. I stood with the others staring anxiously at the pick-up window. After darting back and forth behind the counter, and checking under more shelves, the pharmacist reached for the telephone. He held it to his ear for a long time before calling me over.

"This isn't a single prescription," he said. "This is ten prescriptions. I can't even make half of this out."

"He needs to take one of the medications in an hour," I said. I felt desperate and powerless. There wasn't time to track down the doctor.

"All right, you listen to this," the pharmacist said. He thrust the phone over the counter, along with a slip of paper on which he had scrawled a list of abbreviations and dosages.

I pressed the phone to my ear, straining to catch the doctor's rushed instructions. The scrawled words and numbers on the slip of paper meant nothing to me. What the doctor was saying meant nothing to me. I handed the phone back across the counter and stared at the cramped writing that amounted to medical hieroglyphics.

"It's that last one," the pharmacist said. "I can't tell if it's one refill or two."

"What's standard?"

"Whatever the doctor wants."

"Make it two, then," I said. I thought that was what I had heard.

The pharmacist gave me a long look. "Do you know how much this is going to cost? Does he have coverage for this?"

"No. How much is it going to cost?"

This elicited a heavy sigh. He jotted figures on the scrap of paper. "Five hundred, five hundred and fifty dollars, something like that."

Robert had said nothing to me about payment. I told the pharmacist to wait a minute while I called him.

I went to a corner of the store where bottles of windshield washer fluid were stacked in a display and dialed Robert's number on my cell phone. His phone rang and kept on ringing. I let it go eight times before hanging up. I dialed again. Still no answer. Maybe he had collapsed and couldn't get to the phone. I could think of only one thing: He needed that medication in the next hour. I went back to the pharmacist and told him to fill the prescriptions.

"It'll take at least twenty minutes," he said. His annoyance was moving up a notch with each exchange.

I said I would wait. I slumped into one of the molded plastic chairs, my hands sunk in the pockets of my jacket. It was just after eleven. On an ordinary morning I would be at my desk with the cat curled beside me. Now, under the harsh overhead lighting and the hostile gaze of the pharmacist, it seemed that an entire day had passed already, a day in which I had accomplished nothing. I wanted only to go home and sleep. How, I wondered, did someone like Robert navigate this world? He must have encountered this sort of scorn often. The pharmacist struck me as expressing a distinctly American attitude: Robert, like most of the poor, was responsible for getting himself into the sorry state in which he existed. I was a sap for becoming involved.

I sat there staring at a shelf lined with cans of soup until the pharmacist barked out Robert's name. When I went to the counter, he thrust the slip of paper at me. "This isn't a prescription," he said, indicating a circled item. "It's a nicotine patch. You have to get it at the front counter."

As I turned away, he called after me, "It costs seventy dollars."

His voice carried the clear suggestion that I didn't have the seventy dollars and neither did Robert. I stood for a long moment in front of the pharmacy counter, confused and chagrined. Everyone knew that Robert had stopped smoking. This was part of the story we told about him now, but if the doctor had ordered a nicotine patch, this story was not true. I thought of my recent visits to Robert's apartment. I had never smelled cigarette smoke, never seen an ashtray or a pack of cigarettes, but he was smoking, or the doctor, at least, believed he was.

I went to the front of the store, still struggling to make sense of this. That Robert would smoke on the sly, keeping it from me, was no surprise. There was plenty he kept from me. Smoking was in a different category from his evasiveness about his family and his past, though. It was also an addiction over which, I had to concede, he no doubt had little control.

I scanned the shelves behind the front counter. There were rows of cigarette cartons and then, beside them, several brands of nicotine patches in a glass-fronted case. The brightly colored boxes seemed to be laughing at me, just like the pharmacist. Was I really that naïve? Did I really believe Robert had stopped smoking?

I suspected the doctor had not discussed the nicotine patch with Robert and that he might not use the patches if I purchased them. I couldn't see shelling out seventy dollars for something I was almost certain he would dismiss. I went back to the pharmacy and, after another wait, put four hundred and fifty dollars' worth of drugs on my credit card.

I was not used to being treated as I had been by the pharmacist, but it wasn't just my guilt by association with this man who was dependent on a web of public services. Robert was directly responsible for his illness and was exacerbating the situation with his reckless behavior. The pharmacist's demeaning looks seemed to say that this was a waste of resources and money. Robert was just going to keep smoking.

Back at Robert's apartment, I handed him the bag full of vials and boxes and blister packs. "It cost four hundred and fifty dollars," I said. "I tried to call you, but there was no answer."

His eyes widened in alarm. "I'm sorry. I don't know what happened. I didn't hear the phone ring."

"I put it on my credit card."

"I'll pay you back. That is, when I get my check. I have to get to the bank. Can you wait another week?"

I told him that I could wait; I didn't have to pay my credit card bill for another month.

"I didn't realize it would cost that much," Robert said.

"No, neither did I."

He was embarrassed and flustered. I could have done more to reassure him, but I was still stung and confused myself, and frightened by this new role into which I had been thrust.

"The social worker at the hospital is working on getting coverage for my prescriptions," he said.

"So this will be covered?"

"No. We still have to set it up. But from now on they'll be covered. I can pay you when I've got my disability check."

I told him there was no hurry, but I saw that, for Robert, there was. He was visibly squirming at the thought of being indebted to me.

"The pharmacist was not very helpful," I said.

"No, he's not very helpful." Robert grimaced. "He can be quite abrupt."

I explained about the nicotine patch and how much it cost. "I wasn't sure if you'd want that filled," I said, "so I didn't get it."

Robert furrowed his forehead defiantly. "No, I don't want that."

I had guessed correctly. He was insulted and would not be patronized, by me or the doctor. I had real questions about whether he was going to be able to manage the dosages for the array of drugs I had just handed him. I could not imagine adding the nicotine patch to the mix. I was irritated, too, in the way that the pharmacist had been. If Robert wanted to keep smoking and kill himself faster, who was I to stand in the way?

He asked me if I'd like to stay for tea, but I declined. I had already spent far more time than I intended on the—as I had imagined it—brief errand of bringing him home. I wanted to salvage something from the day.

The next time I visited, Robert presented me with a check for the full amount of the pharmacy bill and told me that he had switched drugstores. The pharmacist at the new store delivered prescriptions to the residents at the Feaster Apartments and would be happy to add Robert to his rounds.

From the notebooks of Robert Dunn

....

*W*hen the North Church steeple blew down (on account of high winds or questionable theology, depending on who you're talking to) people decided at once that Portsmouth simply would not work without a tall steeple in the center of town. So over the next few weeks a web of scaffolding grew up to surround the empty shape of a steeple. The ideal of a steeple. Perfect in itself, as ideals must be.

And now the steeple shape has filled with wood and copper and paint. There's talk of the gilded weathervane going up soon and the clock starting up again. A bit off time as church clocks should be. The steeple becomes a reality, up to a point, and remains an ideal beyond that. Which is a property of steeples.

Which can be a reason for being discomfortable with steeples and the houses underneath them. Many of us can remember signs at nearby resorts saying White Christians Only. I wouldn't much care to be a white Christian only, having known a few, and it's possible that the condition might be catching.

Which brings us to an imperative that steeples raise: that we must respect the values of our neighbors, most especially when we must not share them. As the Irish say, there is good to be found even in an Englishman. (Admittedly they don't say it often.)

Not that we should settle for just being tolerant. The most hideous moments of the last judgment might be the discovery that I had barely tolerated people who are much better than I. It would be such a loss not to delight in the differences. People are strong and weak, wise and foolish, here and there. And if we're not careful we may end up grudgingly tolerating the colors of autumn leaves.

So in the community of poets—a much more raffish lot than the communion of saints—we have Emily Dickinson and Walt Whitman inhabiting the same moment. And as likely as not find ourselves hopelessly in love with both of 'em. The canon of poets easily becomes something like the canon of the mass. "Emily, Walt, stand here beside us."

11.

Vesper Sparrow

On the eastern edge of the country, night comes quickly in winter, bringing a darkness that seems impenetrable by four-thirty in the afternoon. I have never quite become accustomed to setting off for the post office in the dark, swaddled in scarf and gloves. One day that December I had to make the trip by walking in the middle of the street along the river because the sidewalks were covered in mounds of snow left by the first storm of the season. The moon, just coming up, emerged from behind elongated clouds to cast a wispy light.

As I made my way back home, my head was level with windows that allowed me to peer into my neighbors' lives. I passed a young man seated at a computer, so close to the sidewalk that I could have reached out and touched him if the window had been open. He did not turn his head as I went by. I spotted another man in a second-story window, also at the computer, and thought how we are all tethered to our electronic devices day and night now.

Since his hospitalization, Robert had been on steroids and an array of other drugs, one designed to counteract the side effects of the next. The drugs made it possible for him to breathe and eat. He could walk short distances—over to the bank or to the bookstore—but the rest of downtown was out of reach. That night as I covered one of his old routes, the emptiness of the street came home to me. It wasn't just the hour and the silence of winter, and the single figures in the windows bathed in the glow from computer screens. Robert was missing.

Bystanders at heart, writers are practiced in the art of watching. We live each moment twice—as human beings who inhabit these bodies and interact with others, and as writers who note what can be used and file it away. Every story someone tells us is potential material, every overheard conversation possible inspiration. Uncurtained windows are opportunities.

Robert was a practiced observer, his watching honed to a heightened sensitivity. He made Portsmouth his canvas and for thirty years covered these streets with an eye to picking up every unexpected treasure, every small revelation, every window into other lives. The novelist Wallace Stegner, in an essay titled "The Sense of Place," says of Americans: ". . . always hopeful of something better, hooked on change, a lot of us have never stayed in one place long enough to learn it, or have learned it only to leave it." Robert had clearly "learned" Portsmouth.

Robert's fundamental contentment with himself and the world enabled him to see more. He was not, like the rest of us, constantly looking over his shoulder to reevaluate the past or trying to make the future bend to his will. He understood that the search for something better was a false search. Whatever he needed, which wasn't much, could be found right here. This is the mark of real brilliance, to be profoundly engaged with what is simple and ordinary, and to know it as rich beyond measure. Robert worked with a small canvas, secure in the knowledge that there were no limits to what he could do with that canvas. There was always poetry to be found in his daily walks, his stops at the post office and coffee shop, and the scene in Market Square.

There's an irony in our looking to someone like Robert, who deliberately defined himself outside the mainstream of human life, to tell us about the living of that life. This person watching from the sidelines should, it seem, be the least qualified to illuminate our experience, but this is what we ask of writers. The ones who produce the most lasting books are often ruthless at separating themselves from the world. In this riddle lies the uncertainty at the heart of the writer's work. We have no right to make claims for the rest of our human brothers and sisters, but this is precisely what we do. We plant a flag at the summit of human experience. We assert that though we might be quiet, watchful types prone to lurking in corners, we have some insight into the lives of our more active neighbors that gives us the license to tell their stories.

Solitude is not a recipe by itself for good writing, nor does good writing necessarily require solitude, but often when these elements come together at the highest levels, something sublime occurs. Robert is a good example. He was beloved as a poet, among those who knew his work in New Hampshire and beyond, because he had his finger on the pulse of a few significant truths and translated them into language that, though the voice might have been quirky and unpredictable, was instantly recognizable as our own, common language. He stood outside the world while giving it back to us whole.

When Robert became sick, he could no longer keep the careful distance of the observer between himself and the town he had come to know so well. It wasn't just that he could not walk the streets as he once had, but that he was drawn into closer relationships with everyone from his neighbors at the Feaster Apartments to the people who delivered Meals on Wheels. I was included in this web, one of a growing collection of people who came and went from his apartment. Robert and I were shaken from the comfortable stance of the observer and thrust into the business of living in an all too real way. Hiding behind words did not work for us now.

* * *

"I was wondering if you could do a bit of Christmas shopping for me," Robert said when I went to visit one day that December. "I'm afraid I can't make it out to the mall."

The idea that Robert had ever been to the mall was, at best, bizarre, but I knew he had made the trip for my reading and, it appeared, done shopping there at other times. He produced a twenty-dollar bill from the pocket of his baggy corduroys. For a moment, I imagined he was going to ask me to purchase a gift for myself.

"I always get Mrs. Wilson a wall calendar," he said. "One of those Audubon ones. They have them at the bookstore at the mall. If you could get one and take it over to her, I'd much appreciate it."

What had made me think Robert would give me a gift? The idea seemed vain and foolish as I slid the bill into my pocket.

I avoided going to the mall any time of the year, unless it was absolutely necessary. In December, I went to considerable lengths to find gifts that could be purchased elsewhere. I was busy preparing for a Christmas celebration with Jim's family and the arrival of my mother for a week. I was barely able to make time for a visit with Robert; I certainly did not have an extra couple of hours to go out to the mall and deliver the gift to Connie. Naturally I said I would do it.

Robert had engaged me, I recognized, in an odd exercise. We were both going to pretend that he was just like other people who went Christmas shopping and doled out presents. Perhaps this was true, for all I knew, but his request felt like a test. Was I going to deny him this small, ordinary gesture? He might deny himself a great deal, but he would not tolerate others assuming he had no need of the things they did. I was coming to see this as the position Robert often adopted in relation to the world at large. Beneath his gentle and quiet demeanor lay a fierce vigilance. He was just waiting to catch others in the slightest act of belittlement.

I perused the stores downtown, but Robert was right—none of them carried the sort of wall calendar he had instructed me to buy. I made my way to the mall, impatient and annoyed, on a weekday around dinnertime, when I hoped the crowds would be bearable. I called Connie a week before Christmas to ask if I could stop by.

"Oh, yes, Robert always got me a calendar," she said when I explained the nature of my errand. "He didn't need to do it this year. That's really unnecessary."

I agreed with Connie's assessment, but clearly the delivery was necessary to Robert, and I felt in that moment how much he had to prove, and how he was now forced to enlist others in helping him do so. Mrs. Wilson must not be forgotten.

"I'm rather busy," Connie said distractedly. "My daughter's coming to get me tomorrow."

I asked if I could just come by that evening and drop off the gift. She agreed, though there was reluctance in her tone. I walked over to Whidden Street in the lowering light and handed her the calendar through the opened crack in the door. She thanked me, and I went on my way.

"I thought she might be expecting it," Robert said when I went to visit him and reported on the completion of my mission. "I do appreciate your doing that. She's eighty-nine now, you know."

I nodded, silently waiting for more. I still had not shaken the idea that Robert might have a gift for me, but he set the plate of butter cookies on the table without producing anything else.

That day I was consumed with thoughts of all I had to do before my mother's arrival. I tried to still my mind and simply be there,

present with Robert, but I was assaulted by images of the dirty bath-
rooms at home needing to be cleaned and the sheets that had to be
washed. I rattled on in a somewhat oblivious fashion about how we
celebrated Christmas. Robert knew little about my family or Jim's,
I realized, little in fact about how I spent my time when I wasn't at
the desk writing. To Robert I was simply a writer of novels and occasional short stories and poems. The rest of my time was a blank
to him, but now he was learning about my teaching and freelance
work, my sisters and mother and father and niece and nephew, and
the week Jim and I would spend in Florida in February. He seemed
surprised to discover the full dimensions of my life, as I so often was
in what I learned about him.

I mentioned some of my family's Christmas traditions—listening to Dylan Thomas read "A Child's Christmas in Wales" on Christmas Day after opening presents, and tuning in to public radio for
the broadcast of the Christmas Eve service from King's College in
Cambridge.

Robert pressed his fingertips together and smiled. "I always
look forward to that. I have a CD of the service. I listen to it on
Christmas Eve."

I had brought him a jar of raspberry jelly Jim had made and one
of our Christmas cards with a photo of me and Jim and Zane. He
thanked me for these things when I rose to go. Outside, a light snow
was falling. The floodlights that illuminated the parking lot gave the
swirling snow an eerie orange tint. I thought of Robert sitting in
his room listening to the CD of the Christmas Eve service by himself and realized I had never wondered how he passed the holidays.
This seemed like an insensitive oversight of the sort he watched for,
though I didn't think he would have wanted to join my noisy family
for Christmas dinner. As I brushed the snow from the windshield of
my car, I could not shake the image of him seated there with his CD

player. This may have been precisely what he wanted to be doing on Christmas Eve, but to me, that night and in that season, it looked like loneliness.

* * *

"I was thinking I might like to subscribe to *The New Yorker*," Robert said.

We were seated in our usual places, but this afternoon we drank red wine. He had brought the two wineglasses on a tray that rattled in his shaking hands as he crossed the room. I had resisted an urge to jump up and grab it from him.

"It's just that I'm not sure it makes much sense, seeing as I won't be around much longer."

The words lay there between us, unapproachable. I found myself wishing he had not spoken them, because I did not want to talk about what lay ahead, although there was a relief of sorts at having it named.

I held his gaze for a long moment before answering. Behind his horn-rimmed glasses, his eyes were steady and surrendered. I marveled, as I had before, at his calm, matter-of-fact acceptance.

"I can bring you the issues when we're through with them, that is if I can find them in the house," I said. "They tend to get buried under piles of stuff."

"I appreciate the offer, but I rather like reading the magazine when it comes out."

"Then you should subscribe to it. Why not?"

"I just thought it might be a lot of bother for someone one of these days, having to deal with canceling subscriptions and so forth."

"I wouldn't worry about that. If you want the magazine, you might as well get it."

"Perhaps you're right." Robert delivered these words in a low murmur I could barely catch.

His mumbled response did not leave me certain I had persuaded him, but on a subsequent visit, I spotted the latest issue of *The New Yorker* on his desk.

In the months that followed, "call Robert" remained a constant item on the list of daily tasks I scribbled on the back of used envelopes. I would draw a black line through the words and, within hours, add them to the next list. I learned to call in the evening because often he was not in his apartment in the afternoon. He was in the hallway then with the other residents of the Feaster Apartments or outside on the bench in good weather.

The conversations that took place while I was preparing dinner or loading the dishwasher became oddly routine, awkward and wonderful at the same time. We talked about birds, a passion of mine, and the latest snowstorm and the ongoing madness of the war in Iraq, remaining on the phone for half an hour, even longer sometimes. Once when I mentioned the challenge of shoveling the frozen walkway to the house, Robert suggested using fireplace ashes. He made other comments about gardening and canning the harvest that indicated he had some familiarity with country life, though he seemed so removed from it now. He often made me laugh with his comments about the state of the world and our peculiar corner of it (he was good at lampooning New Hampshire). I made him laugh by repeating things Jim said, like the fact that we had enough carbon credits to last the rest of our lives because we didn't have children. Unfailingly polite, Robert never gave signs of having anything else to do when I called. There were nights when I felt he kept talking because he thought that was what I wanted, and others, when I strained to find a topic, that it seemed he was the one who did not want to hang up.

His illness and living situation made Robert accessible to others as he had never been before. He accepted this new state with great equanimity, even seemed to welcome it, but there were times I sensed that he put up with the phone calls and visits because he had no choice. The daily intrusion of people was part of the bargain he had made to stay alive.

Meals on Wheels now delivered a meal at noon Mondays through Fridays. One of these meals supplied enough food, he told me, for days, and the lack of deliveries on the weekend was a welcome break. Nonetheless, he seemed happy to have this matter settled. He no longer had to worry about taking the senior citizen van to the store. A home health aide came at least once a week to clean and run errands. The steroids and other medications were clearly making a difference. When I visited, I found him, as he would put it, "in fine fettle," his eyes bright, his skin less sallow, his spirit on good days buoyant.

* * *

My cat Zane, like Robert, seemed to know he had been given a second chance. We had almost made the decision to put Zane to sleep, at the vet's suggestion, when another doctor urged us to try a daily dose of steroids. Robert and I had discussed the marvel of these drugs that were keeping both him and my cat alive. Now Zane had spent an entire year not just in remission but with a new vigor. The steroids kept the cancer in check while making his arthritic joints more supple. Our fifteen-year-old cat was once again leaping up onto the bed and dresser, and racing across the backyard.

I experienced many moments in that year when I looked into Zane's eyes and saw a profound gratitude in the gaze he fixed on me. It would be easy to dismiss this as simply a projection of my own gratitude, and perhaps this was all these moments amounted to, but I had a stronger sense than ever of communicating with him on a deep, unspoken level. He seemed to understand that something was wrong and that I was trying to help him. The knowledge that he would not be with us much longer made me notice not just him but everything I loved more. Zane could be gone at any time, in a week or a month, we didn't know, but for today, he was still here, and this was the cause of a happiness that at times felt almost unbearable, linked as it was with the certainty of loss. Just in time, it seemed, I had recognized how much I shared with this cat, how much he meant to me. His illness, near death, and remission had given me something unaccountably precious: the ability to meet the loss with my eyes open, fully knowing what it would mean while fully holding the present close.

I think of those months now as a time of terrific joy and terrific pain, one tied inextricably to the other. They were like the final days of fall when the saturation of the sunlight and the last vibrant leaves left on the trees are too brilliant, it seems, to be real. I was reminded at every turn, as I am on those fall days, that this staggering sense of wonder, this brightness, would not last and reminded, too, to cling to it as long as I could, to savor every moment.

In many ways, these days with Zane were a dress rehearsal for what would come with Robert, though, as I would discover, the course of a human illness is so much more complicated, buffeted by anxiety and conflict.

* * *

In the spring, Zane stopped eating again. He went into a quick decline, and it was clear, after only a few days, that there would be no rebounding this time. We took him to the vet and made the decision to have him put to sleep. We had not opted for treatment of the cancer other than the steroids and had decided against surgery, which would have determined whether he was suffering from colon or stomach cancer without making much difference. We did not regret any of the decisions we had made. The final year of his life had been a time of unexpected happiness.

Zane had been with us since our move to Portsmouth and marriage. He was the only pet I had lived with like this, over a period of so many years. In the weeks after his death, I often reflected that I had spent more time with him than I had with Jim. He had been beside me throughout the day, a constant companion, and the house felt like a hollow, abandoned shell without him.

On a morning shortly after his death, when I was still in a wandering state of grief, the phone rang.

"Oh, Katie," Robert said when I answered, as if he had been expecting someone else. "I'm afraid I'm in some difficulty."

"What's wrong?" He seldom called, even now, and I assumed he was back in the hospital.

There was a long pause before he answered. "I'm having a bit of trouble breathing. The doctor called in a prescription yesterday, but it was too late for the delivery, and now they won't deliver again until Monday."

"So it needs to be picked up?"

"Yes, that's the thing. I was wondering . . ." He trailed off.

"I can get it for you."

"I'm sorry to bother you."

"That's all right. I can bring it by."

His voice, so soft and hesitant, was laced with desperation. I felt how much it had taken him to make this request. I could rearrange my Saturday.

I had not been to the new pharmacy where Robert now did his business. The pharmacist greeted me with a cheery hello. "How is Mr. Dunn?" he asked when I explained why I was there.

"He's doing all right. He's at home."

"That's good. I saw him a few weeks ago."

"He appreciates the deliveries."

"I'm sorry I don't have enough coverage to do them on the weekends." The pharmacist handed me a small paper bag with the prescription stapled to it. "There's a one-dollar co-pay for that."

"Oh, Robert didn't mention it." I fished in my purse for a bill.

"Sometimes they forget at the Feaster Apartments or they don't have a dollar. I just toss in a dollar if I have to." He smiled, as if to say he knew I understood.

I felt a kinship with the pharmacist out of proportion with our small exchange as I made my way to the car. I was so grateful for his kindness, for the simple fact of his treating me, and Robert, as fellow human beings.

Portsmouth, NH
March 14, 2006

Dear Katie,

After you left from your errand of mercy, I realized that I had neglected to pay for the prescription. Now that will never do. Fortunately it's easy to remedy.

The stuff seems to be working (whew!) although slowly (grumble, grumble) so the effort was worthwhile.

I hope you and Jim are healing also. Zane should make a good memory for you as time passes.

Cheers,
Robert

Included with this letter was a dollar bill and a Xerox copy of the
following poem:

Vesper sparrow, turnable of bellbirds,
the small owls have called from tree to tree.
No need to comfort or be comforted.
Pitched high or low, grief is a kind of love
and so must be. Or no one else will know
when the sparrow falls, least of all the sparrow.

—Robert Dunn

12.

A Crafted Life

Publication, I had always imagined, would be the answer to a host of frustrations that had plagued me for years. That elusive recognition would be mine at last, and with it would come time to write. I would be able to quit all my day jobs and sit around wallowing in my own brilliance. Naturally, what awaited me as a published writer was pretty much the polar opposite of this fantasy. It quickly became clear that I would have even less time for writing. Being an author was another job added to the ones I already had, and I wasn't making enough money to quit any of them.

More disconcerting than this realization, though, was something I had not even thought about: a new and very public identity, one that was out of my hands and beyond my control. People read my book and felt they knew me when they did not know me at all. I could not get used to the idea that I, who had become a writer because I was such a private person, had done something so brazenly public.

Writers have something to say and want to be heard, but many of us are not good at going out in public. Writing, that private act, is a way of being public without actually facing people. For me, writing had always been, whether I articulated it to myself or not, a path to becoming known without having to traffic in the common stuff others did to become successful in the eyes of the world. I could make my mark while remaining quiet and shy and solitary. The words on the page would proclaim what I had accomplished for me. I didn't need to be good at anything besides imagining fully realized characters and shaping stories and sentences. It seemed like a perfect arrangement, until I understood, after getting published, that the words on the page were only the beginning and, in the current age, were not enough. Unwittingly, it seemed, I had committed myself to being a public person. What I had always wanted, or thought I had wanted, had the potential, I quickly realized, to rob me of what I most loved, the solitude that made the writing possible.

In a piece published in *The New York Times Book Review* a few years before his death, John Updike noted that in the first twenty years of his career as a published writer, he was almost never asked to address audiences or give readings. In those less commercial days in American life, the writer was not expected to do more than write. The words on the page were all one needed, beyond the jacket photo and a brief biography. How innocent, and sane, such an attitude seems now.

In the age of Facebook and Twitter, we have turned into a nation of self-promoters. Woe to the writer who does not join the mad frenzy of constant status updates. Privacy has become more or less a dead concept. A published writer who wants to maintain privacy is hopelessly old school, ridiculous and quaint, crazy even.

If I were Thomas Pynchon—or Robert Dunn—I might have resisted this part of the equation of being an "author," but although staying in his house might have been an option for John Updike, such a refusal on the part of a new writer today (young did not apply in my case, but I was new) would be seen as tantamount to suicide.

In the twenty-first century, it was not possible simply to sit in one's house and write, unless you rocketed to instant stardom or were made of stronger stuff than I was.

When I visited Robert, I sensed that he shared my dismay. He withheld any comments, simply nodded his head and made murmuring sounds of a sympathetic nature, but I heard the unspoken question behind his steady eyes. What really matters here? His frustration showed when I talked about the business of writing (as if it could ever be a "business"). An undercurrent of annoyance emanated from him at my frantic anxiety and my rushed embrace of all the promotional stuff. He was like an owl slowly rotating his head to take me in, the completeness of his gaze unsettling. In that unfettered look there was just a hint of accusation. I had not been able to let go of the craving for recognition that drives our cultural life in America, and this was so clearly not good for me or my writing. Had I forgotten, his look seemed to say, what the writing was about to begin with, a celebration of wonder, and turned it into a job, or worse a career? Had I begun to call myself an Author with a capital A, instead of being someone who writes and lives in a seaside town and wanders its beautiful streets?

From the first days I observed him in Portsmouth, I had been fascinated by how Robert somehow managed to combine being a private and public person. Everyone knew him downtown, and in some ways he was more social than I was. He took great pleasure in following the latest controversies, such as whether the parking rate should be raised to seventy-five cents an hour. This controversy would have no impact on him. He simply enjoyed the extent to which people got worked up about things of relatively little consequence.

I often wished that I had made a different bargain, more like the one Robert had made. He had managed to get his poems out there while sidestepping the whole business of being a writer. He was a public person in the little world of Portsmouth, a scale that suited him. He was personally acquainted with many of his readers and cared not a whit what they thought of his poems. How I admired the freedom this gave him.

Robert's ambition was for the carefully crafted life as much as it was for the poetry. He framed the equation on his own terms, though. He sent his poems out and was glad when they found readers, but he set himself apart from the "poetry biz," that great, overblown realm of prizes and accolades and cutthroat competition. He had thrown off the yoke of that ambition. In this respect, he was something like the Chinese poet Li Po, of the Tang Dynasty, who wrote his poems on scraps of paper, folded them into little boats, and sent them down the river without caring whether they were read or not.

What I saw most clearly as I sat drinking the tea or wine Robert placed before me was this: He did not believe the world owed him anything. He was ruled by a measured, tranquil acceptance; I was like a moth trapped behind glass, struggling to get out. He thought about what he could give back, while I was consumed by what sometimes felt like a fury about what the world owed me and had not yet delivered.

* * *

In the summer of 2006, I started a new teaching job at Southern New Hampshire University that required I live in a dorm room on campus for ten days at the end of July. About to turn fifty, I went back to sleeping in a narrow single bed on a foam mattress covered with a plastic pad that made a loud, crackling complaint every time I turned over and drank beer with my colleagues in the hallway out of a cup so we wouldn't get busted by the twenty-year-old resident advisor for bringing alcohol into the dorm.

My new job meant that I was away even more than I had been in the past. Mimi, Anne, Nancy, and Liz, all people connected to the Poet Laureate Program, checked on Robert and sent me updates. He was settled back into a routine and seemed to be doing all right.

I drove to book events in Massachusetts and Maine hoping for a break in the weather. It was turning out to be the third hottest summer on record in New England. Like many people in this part of the country, I tend to review the forecast frequently. You never know when a sudden shift in the weather may occur. In my obsession with studying the radar map, as in other things, I have become a victim of access to too much information. If I can amass enough information—which, thanks to the Internet and my array of electronic devices, I certainly can, in a constant, overwhelming stream—maybe I can begin to feel I have a measure of control over this crazy world I inhabit. With enough information, I might even be able to shape the course of future events, or at least convince myself that I can do so. All too quickly, though, the accumulation of all this data becomes immobilizing. Instead of taking action, I stare dumbly at the screen.

On my visits with Robert, we talked about the computer and the changes it had brought to people's lives. He listened in wide-eyed amusement as I explained how one could now access the Internet almost anywhere. "I don't think I will ever try one of those things," he said on more than one occasion about the computer. There wasn't much regret in his voice.

He listened to the radio, NPR mostly, and got his daily delivery of newspapers from Richard. In addition to *The New Yorker*, he now subscribed to *Poetry* magazine and *The Sun*, which he had discovered when someone brought a copy to him in the hospital. This was more than enough information for Robert.

* * *

One week when I was home for a few days, Mimi called. "Robert needs an air conditioner," she said. "He can't breathe in the humidity. Do you think we could take up a collection and buy him one?"

"I'll contribute," I said. "One window unit would probably do the whole apartment." I told her I would discuss it with Robert.

My obsession with the weather had a new focus now. The heat was more than an annoyance and inconvenience. I watched the numbers—humidity percentage, heat index, climbing temperatures—and wondered if Robert would land back in the hospital. In my busy oblivion, the impact of the heat on him had not even occurred to me until Mimi mentioned it.

"Some of us were thinking it might be a good idea to get an air conditioner for you," I said to Robert when I found time to visit.

Before I had even finished the sentence, he drew his shoulders up defiantly. I saw my mistake. I should not have begun with "some of us were thinking."

"I don't want an air conditioner," he said stiffly. "That is unnecessary."

He spoke as if I had suggested something absurd and slightly obscene, like buying him a Rolls-Royce. An air conditioner? This was the height of indulgence and extravagance.

"How about a fan at least?" He did not even have this "luxury."

He shook his head. "I think not. I don't get the sun on the windows here, except early in the morning. It's not that hot, really."

His apartment felt a good five to ten degrees cooler than out on the sidewalk, but I would not have gone so far as to claim that it was not hot. I changed the topic.

Mimi gave me a grave look when I reported back to her. "Breathing that air puts a strain on his lungs," she said.

"I know. He was adamant."

She clucked her tongue. "He's one stubborn man."

I smiled. "Stubborn and wonderful."

We gazed at each other before moving on to something else, and in that exchange lay the unspoken understanding that we were lucky to know this confounding person.

A week later when I was home again, I bought a fan at the drugstore and took it to Robert. We were suffering through another heat wave, with the temperature hovering around ninety for most of the day. Robert drew back when I presented the fan, but after a moment, he took it from me. I had purchased a simple table fan that rotated when you pushed a button. As fans go, it was quite small and unobtrusive.

"How much did it cost?" Robert asked when we were seated in the armchairs, glasses of white wine beside us.

"You don't need to pay me for it."

"Certainly I do."

"It was twenty dollars."

He got up from the chair, went to the table that served as his desk, and extracted a worn leather wallet from a pile of papers and pill bottles. I took the bill he handed me, wondering if he would actually use the fan. He did not turn it on while I was in the apartment, though the air was thick enough to slice and serve on a plate.

The next time I spoke with Robert on the phone, he said, "Oh, by the way, that fan has come in quite handy. It really makes a difference."

* * *

Jim and I had decided to ignore our fiftieth birthdays, which were rapidly approaching. Born a week apart in the same year, we joked when we first met that we were twins separated at birth. Now we were turning fifty together, an event that struck us as completely unexplainable and not worth calling to anyone's attention. Some friends of ours were having none of this, though, and planned a party to be held at the spacious home of another couple. When they asked us for an invitation list, I included Robert.

Jim and I drove to Robert's apartment the night of the party. He was dressed in his usual uniform of chinos, button-down shirt, and corduroy jacket. We made the fifteen-minute drive with him hunched in the front seat looking a bit like a gnome.

The living room was festooned with balloons hanging from the ceiling and a banner wishing us a happy fiftieth. We were a bit early, and only a few people had arrived. Robert slid into a straight-backed chair over in a corner and took in the scene. As people trickled in, he seemed content to remain in his place observing the action without speaking to anyone, as if he had determined that his presence was all that was called for.

I brought him a glass of wine and asked if he would like me to get him a plate of food. He said he wasn't feeling up to eating anything. The wine would do.

As I circulated through the room greeting people, I could not shake the awareness of Robert over there in the corner, silent and alone. He looked smaller in this crowd, thin as a piece of paper, and completely out of place. I wondered what he thought of the beautifully decorated house and the overflowing platters of food. Through his eyes, it struck me as excessive, though Robert gave no indication of having such thoughts himself.

A few people went over and made the attempt to speak with him. The conversations did not last long. I could see that they strained to catch what he was saying and quickly gave up. This did not appear to bother Robert in the least. He had come to the party, I realized, for me, not for himself, and I was touched.

A couple of those present at the party were longtime Portsmouth residents who knew Robert as well as anyone in town did. One of them pulled a chair up next to his and remained there for a good fifteen minutes. For that interlude, Robert did not seem quite so stranded.

An hour or more had passed, and Robert had consumed his glass of wine. One of the longtime residents offered to drive him home. When I saw him getting unsteadily to his feet, I went over. "It was a lovely party," he said. "But I think I'll be going."

I thanked him for coming and watched Robert follow our mutual friend slowly to the door, his pace revealing how tired he was. Inviting Robert now struck me as a selfish mistake, a misguided attempt to integrate him into this other life I led, a life filled with people and an overabundance of gifts and food and music and noise. I felt sad for both of us as he trailed out the door. Our essential selves were lost in this mob scene, though perhaps, I considered on further reflection, everyone in that room experienced some measure of dislocation between who they were in a social situation and who they knew themselves to be at home, alone. Seated in his corner chair, quietly present without feeling the need to participate, Robert had been the embodiment of this dislocation, a reminder that no matter how enthusiastically we adopted our social personas and presented a unified version of ourselves to others, we would return to more complex truths when the night was over.

* * *

A week after the fiftieth birthday party, I received the following note on stationery decorated with multicolored balloons. A handwritten copy of a poem was included.

Wishing you a good recovery from all the partyfication.

Cheers,
Robert

Received Wisdom

If you're ever chased by a bear
run downhill.
Bears don't run very fast
going downhill.
       So they say.
Let me know, if you can
how it works out.
I don't think there's any real need
to bring the bear.

—Robert Dunn

Robert wrote this poem in response to the story I told him about a
bear who had visited our yard in Vermont.

III.

Walking to Windward

13.

Conjured from the Air

With the coming of fall, I traveled less and returned to the routine of calling Robert in the evenings. I did not begin by asking how he was feeling. That would have been too direct and might succeed in getting only an evasive response. I waited until we had discussed the latest absurdities in Washington or the books we were reading. Once we had meandered over various topics, I would slip in one or two of my "check-up" questions. Was he getting the deliveries from Meals on Wheels? Was the home health aide still coming? How was his breathing?

One night in early November, Robert said, "I have an appointment to see the doctor this week."

I sensed that he offered this information in an attempt to placate me.

"When is the appointment?"

"Thursday afternoon."

I glanced at my calendar. I had my own doctor's appointment at three-thirty. "What time?" I asked.

"I believe it's at one-thirty." A hint of annoyance was creeping into his voice. He did not like to answer these questions.

"Do you need a ride?"

There was a pause while he seemed to consider the options. "That would be quite helpful," he said finally.

Robert was waiting just inside the lobby when I came to pick him up. I watched as he made his way slowly toward the car. I didn't go around to open the door, hesitant to make him feel incapable. There was such pride and determination in his measured walk.

He managed to open the door and lower himself slowly into the seat. His breathing was labored, but his breathing was always labored. I had grown used to the rattle of the air going in and out of his lungs.

I chattered away as we made the ten-minute drive to the medical complex. I gave him news of writers in town and talked about my family's Thanksgiving plans. Robert made brief responses. He was not as relaxed and cheerful as usual. I understood. I didn't like going to the doctor, either.

At the entrance to the medical complex, he climbed unsteadily from the car. I found a parking space not far from the entrance and reached the main door just as he did. It had taken him that long to make it up the walk. Inside, I matched my pace to his with small steps.

We sat next to each other in the row of chairs along one wall in the doctor's waiting room. Robert looked weaker here, and shabbier, and this made me indignant and sad.

The nurse appeared within minutes of our arrival and called Robert. I remained in the waiting room. A few minutes later, a large man who appeared to be in his fifties emerged from the narrow hallway leading to the examining rooms and took a seat. The round bowl of his belly heaved up and down with each breath. He looked at me and shook his head, as if making a point in a conversation we had already begun. "Doc says I gotta stop smoking," he said.

I nodded.

"I done everything—gone to a course, done the patch, everything. I just can't stop. I want to stop, believe me. But it don't stick."

"It's hard," I said, aware of the utterly lame tone in my voice.

"I'm going to be on oxygen soon if I can't lick this," he said.

I responded with a frown that I hoped indicated my compassion. I was still trying to think of something to say when Robert appeared. He stopped at the desk and handed the receptionist a sheet of paper, then turned to me. I told the man to have a nice day before following Robert to the door.

"So what did the doctor say?" I asked.

He waved a small square of paper in the air. "Gave me a new prescription."

"Good," I said, trying to put a positive spin on whatever had gone on inside the examining room.

When we reached the main door, I noticed how hard Robert was breathing and how slowly he was walking. I said I would get the car. I brought the car around, and he rose from the bench where he had been waiting. It seemed to take forever for him to reach me. This time I went around and opened the door. His chest was heaving up and down, his spare frame shaking.

I started up the car. "Are you all right?" I said.

"No," he gasped. "Take me to the hospital."

I turned to him questioningly. "I can take you back to the doctor."

"The hospital. Now."

He spat *now* out with as much vehemence as his strangled voice could summon. There was terror in that single word.

I shot across the road to the hospital. Neither of us spoke. I drove as fast as I dared, which was not fast enough. We circled the hospital to the emergency room entrance at the rear, the seconds stretched out longer than seemed possible, like drops of water falling in slow motion from a leaky faucet.

I pulled up to the double-glass doors and jumped out. Inside, I found the waiting room empty and no one at the desk behind a plate glass window. When I rang the bell, a nurse in one of those brightly patterned smocks and baggy blue scrub pants appeared.

"I've got Robert Dunn here," I said. "It's an emergency. He can't breathe. He's out in the car."

The EMTs were there instantly. I ran beside them down the corridor. They loaded Robert into a wheelchair and whisked him inside. Together we ran back to the waiting room. I stopped when they disappeared through another set of doors that opened and closed automatically.

Back outside, I found my car with the passenger door open and engine still running. I moved it to the parking area and sat there staring through the windshield at the clouds scudding overhead. I felt overwhelmed and inadequate. We had been lucky this time to be across the street from the hospital. What if something like this happened again? I had never been good at responding quickly to anything, whether it was a cutting comment someone made (I would come up with a retort twenty-four hours later) or an emergency. The situation felt dangerous and out of control, and I seemed completely unsuited to handling it.

When I went back inside, the nurse told me they had Robert on oxygen and were getting him stabilized. She made it sound like a routine situation, nothing to be overly alarmed about. I said I would be back and went on to my doctor's appointment.

An hour later, another nurse led me through a maze of corridors. Robert raised his hand weakly as I stepped into the room where he lay on a gurney, a skimpy hospital gown draped over his chest. Uncovered, his bare legs, all bone, shone like the bald head of a newborn. I slipped into a chair beside the gurney with the uncomfortable realization that I could not look at Robert without taking in his gaunt body. Without the covering of his baggy clothes, the sight was unnerving.

Oxygen tubes protruded from his nose and ran to a machine beside the bed. He was hooked up to a heart monitor, with an IV running into one arm.

"You're breathing better," I said.

"Yes. I think we got here just in time." He gave me a rueful smile. "I've got a collapsed lung, they tell me."

I took in this news. "The doctor didn't notice this when you were in the office?"

"Apparently not."

I questioned him about what exactly the doctor had done. He said he had listened to his chest and thought Robert was doing okay.

"I'm not too impressed with that doctor," I said.

"Neither am I."

"Has he been informed?"

"I think the doctor here may have had some words with him."

"So who's going to monitor you now?"

"The doctor who was on call when I came in."

"And the other guy?"

"We'll see. I'm sorry if I gave you a bit of a scare."

I nodded. "It wasn't your fault. That doctor shouldn't have let you leave the office."

"No, I guess not. So how was your appointment?" Robert asked this in the cheery, deflecting tone I had grown used to. He was going to normalize our arrival at this perhaps predictable but still unlikely place, meeting over a gurney, his unclothed body and a maze of wires the centerpiece of our conversation.

I gave a vague account of my appointment. I was having my own medical problems, but they paled in comparison to his, and as much as we had shared, I was not prepared to discuss my visit to the gynecologist. This constraint, like others, threw the situation into bizarre relief. I should, it seemed, have felt closer to Robert.

Our conversation over the next twenty minutes remained muted, tinged with the awareness of how close he might have come this time to not making it. The adrenaline drained out of me, I felt white and empty, the color of Robert's skin. The fluorescent lights flickering overhead made the room cavernous. I addressed him across a gulf of fear and silence, a gulf that represented life itself. I was on one side of that gulf, and he was on the other, but we were both still present, and we met this reality with a stunned and grateful slowness, a pained yet happy amazement.

A nurse appeared and told us that Robert would be transferred to a room upstairs as soon as one was ready. She rotated on one heel and disappeared into the buzz of activity out in the corridor.

"I imagine you have things to do," Robert said.

"I guess I need to think about making dinner."

"Yes, I'm sure you do. Thank you for being a proxy ambulance driver."

I smiled. "It was the least I could do."

"Or the most."

"Are you sure you're going to be all right?"

"Oh, yes, they'll take care of me here. I'll be a bit more comfortable once I get up to the room."

"I'll give you a call tomorrow."

"That would be nice." He raised his head ever so slightly, a gesture of both acknowledgment and dismissal.

I placed my hand on his shoulder for a moment and rose to go. There was barely anything beneath the thin gown to touch.

As I exited through the glass doors, this time at a walk rather than a run, I saw that darkness had fallen. I climbed into the car with the sense that I had entered another time, entirely separate from the day with which this trip had begun. I felt a piercing tenderness for my former self, the woman who had blithely set off to deliver Robert to the doctor's and bring him home. She existed in a simpler world than the one I inhabited now. I couldn't recall Robert marooned on that gurney, stripped down to nothing, without thinking that his dignity, and our friendship, had been violated. The situation forced us into an intimacy that felt foreign. We had taken another step in an involvement neither of us had quite sought or even agreed to. I was grateful in some ways, dismayed in others. What I appeared to have signed up for, without realizing it, was much more than visiting a sick acquaintance. Our friendship had begun to feel like a relationship outside definition of any kind, an unaccountable marriage of sorts.

I drove the road away from the hospital and wondered if I should have stayed until they took him up to a room, but he hadn't seemed to want this. Still, I felt heartless leaving him there alone. I reminded myself, as I had many times before, that Robert had chosen his solitude a long time ago, before we met. Though maybe he needed family now, I wasn't sure that even in these extreme circumstances he wanted family, and I couldn't produce one out of thin air in any case. He and I would have to be satisfied with what I was able to do, which so often did not feel like enough.

* * *

Following the trip to the emergency room, Robert was on a mechanical ventilator. When I visited, he was off the ventilator, but he couldn't speak much and indicated that the process of getting hooked up to the ventilator was extremely painful. The doctor had botched the procedure somehow, making the pain worse. He was heavily medicated and dopey.

Jim and I stopped to visit on our way back from Thanksgiving dinner with Jim's family in Massachusetts and brought a bag of books with us. The lung was healing, but Robert was still weak, sunk back on a pile of pillows. He rallied, though, and entertained us as though we were seated in his apartment with a glass of cheap wine.

The social worker called a few days later. "He's going to have to go to rehab," she said. "You need to visit the nursing homes in the area and decide where he should be discharged."

This was a daunting assignment. How could I make such a decision? It felt, too, like the crossing of another boundary.

"How many nursing homes are there?" I asked, stalling for time as I searched for a way to tell her I couldn't do this.

She went over the options. There were just two in Portsmouth that would accept a Medicare patient. Others would be a longer drive. I rejected the ones in outlying towns. The social worker said she couldn't make any recommendations, but she thought the location was probably important. Wouldn't Robert like to be close to the neighborhood he knew?

Yes, I responded, seizing this small nudge of guidance. He would like to be somewhere familiar to him. This narrowed the choice to one facility close to downtown.

"It depends on whether they have a bed available, of course," she said. "But I think they do."

I needed more information, and I could not count on Robert giving it to me. "How long do you think he has to live?" I asked.

"Two to three weeks," she said.

She made this pronouncement with a matter-of-fact certainty that was shocking and at the same time welcome. I wanted the truth, and she had given it to me. I wanted to be prepared. Knowing that this was the end, I would be ready to do whatever Robert needed. I would be ready to treasure every moment left.

* * *

I steeled myself in the days that followed, feeling sad, regretful, and afraid, but prepared. I would face Robert's death with him.

At the hospital, he was seated in the raised bed with the oxygen tubes looped over his ears and running into his nose. This apparatus was disconcerting, but after a few minutes I became used to it. A bit of the old whimsy shone in his eyes.

"You're looking better," I said as I took the chair by the bed.

"So they tell me. I've had a rather steady stream of visitors."

"Are they tiring you out?"

"Oh, no. It's good to have news of the world."

He told me who had been to visit, at least the names of those I knew. Word had gotten around that this hospitalization might be his last. When Robert was done with this recitation, I said, "The social worker tells me they want to send you to rehab."

"Yes, there's been some talk of that."

"There are two places in town. You need to choose one of them."

Robert raised his eyebrows. "I didn't know a choice was involved."

"Yes. There's Edgewood—you know where that is."

He nodded.

"And another place out by the highway."

"As I recall, Esther was quite happy with Edgewood," he said. "I guess that's where I should go." He offered this assessment with a finality that signaled the matter was settled.

I did not remember that Esther Buffler had spent time at Edgewood. This was a good omen.

"She said she got excellent care there," he added.

"All right, then. I'll tell the social worker it will be Edgewood."

Robert nodded, as if he was pleased with both of us for navigating this decision so quickly. No sense in complicating it, he seemed to be saying. He gave no indication he was aware of a timeline for his approaching death, and neither did I.

186 — The Penny Poet of Portsmouth

A wall of heat met me as I stepped through the main entrance of the nursing home. I loosened the scarf around my neck. A woman sat at a piano in the lobby playing "Jingle Bells." She was surrounded by residents, some pulled up beside her in wheelchairs, others perched on couches arranged to give the impression of a living room, though even in their brightly patterned fabrics, these pieces of furniture could not shake an institutional look. Many of the men and women ranged around the piano gazed off at the corners of the room as if they couldn't hear the music.

In the hallway that led to Robert's wing, I threaded my way through residents and aides. One woman who lay prone in a bed with her eyes closed let out a low moan as I passed. Another woman slumped back in a wheelchair, swaddled in blankets with a wool cap pulled down over her head, called out hello. I would come to understand in subsequent visits that Edgewood was a remarkably relaxed and social facility. Residents were not confined to their rooms; one even had a dog. There was a certain energy to the place, despite the hollow-eyed look of many of the people lining the corridors.

Even so, Robert clearly did not belong here. When I entered his room, I found him in the far bed by the window. His roommate, stretched out in the other bed asleep, had the frail, lost appearance of someone just barely in this world, while Robert was sitting up, reading.

"Hello, Katie," Robert called out. He gave me his old smile. Everything about his posture as I pulled a chair up beside the bed told me that there was no need to make anything of this new arrangement.

"How are you getting settled?" I asked.

"Well enough. Everyone is quite agreeable. I'm afraid I may be getting addicted to that thing, though." He gestured toward the small television that dangled at the end of an arm protruding from the wall. "It's quite amazing what's on it. Appalling, actually."

"What have you been watching?"

"The news, and some movies. I watched that *American Idol* show for a couple of minutes."

"That's all I've ever watched of it. I couldn't stand any more."

"It seems to appeal to the worst in people. But then much of what's on TV does." In the hospital, he had managed to ignore the television. Only if he had a roommate would it be turned on. Now, with the set hanging in front of his face, he had given in.

We talked about the issue of *Poetry* he had been reading and the latest political news. On this visit, and the ones that would follow, we created a small oasis in the unlikely setting of the nursing home. Or perhaps I should say that he created the oasis, for he was the one who set the tone of our conversation. There would be no uncalled-for gravity, no feeling sorry for him, no complaining. We would laugh often. Our talk would move from the mundane (the forecast for snow, my Christmas preparations) to what mattered to us most (a poem of W.H. Auden's) and back again. The reassurance that this was just one more place to be came from Robert. With his sly observations and subtle jokes, he projected a magnanimous grace. I knew I would not have his patience and presence if our roles were reversed. For this is what he projected most of all: a profound sense of presence. Despite the tubes running into his nose and the dull hum of the oxygen machine doing its work, he was fully there. He held me in his gaze as if we had all the time in the world. There was nothing to fight or deny, nothing to fear.

That day after forty-five minutes of pleasant talk, I rose to go.

"Oh, I was wondering," Robert said, "if you could go to my apartment and get some clothes. I'm a little sick of wearing this." He gestured at the johnny and the cotton robe covering it.

He made the request as if it had just occurred to him, though I could tell he had spent the last forty-five minutes preparing to voice it. I was instantly aware of my inadequacy as a caretaker. I should have realized he needed clothes.

"You'll find everything in the dresser in the bedroom, and there are some pants and shirts in the closet," he said. "There's a little suitcase on wheels there. That might make it easy to bring everything."

"What do you want me to get?"

"A couple of pairs of pants, and three shirts, I guess. Five pairs of underwear and five socks. Oh, and my slippers. These things are slightly ridiculous." He pointed at the bright blue hospital socks pulled up to his shins. "The slippers should be by the bed. I think that's where I left them. Or maybe in the living room."

He told me to take his keys from the pocket of the jacket hanging in the closet. I did so and said I would be back the next day. At each step in the transaction, Robert was ahead of me. He had clearly given careful thought to the requests he needed to make.

"The key to the mailbox is there, too," he said as I slipped the keys in my purse. "I expect it may be getting a little full. And there's one other thing. I was wondering if you could make a deposit at the bank for me. I got a very large check from Social Security that's sitting on the desk. I'd feel better if that were taken care of."

He said I would find the deposit slips for the bank, which was just a block from his apartment, in a folder on the desk.

* * *

The black, cloying scent of nicotine greeted me inside the apartment. I reached for the light switch, sick with disappointment. So this was the dangerous game Robert was playing. After the hospitalization a year earlier, when the doctor prescribed the nicotine patch, I had assumed that he had learned his lesson. There had been no evidence in recent months that he was smoking, but now I discerned a pattern in the hospitalizations of the past two years. After each one, he must have let his lungs recover, then taken up the cigarettes again. I felt pity more than anger or blame. If his aim was to kill himself, he was succeeding at it.

The table he had purchased at Rite Aid was strewn with prescription bottles and blister packs of pills. His writing desk had become a pharmacy. Newspapers were scattered about the floor by his easy chair. In the kitchen, dirty plates and glasses rimmed with what looked like orange juice sat on the counter. I spotted the salt and pepper shakers in the shape of watering cans I had given him on the windowsill. I had never noticed them there before, though they had probably been decorating the sill all along, for this is what he had obviously done with them, used them for decoration rather than their intended purpose. They struck me as poignant sitting there because Robert had so few personal mementoes in his apartment, so little decoration of any kind.

I surveyed the place as though taking it in for the last time. I did not think Robert would be returning to this apartment. The easy chairs disgorging their stuffing, the dirty dishes, and the bottles of pills spoke of the meagerness of what he had now, not much time and so few comforts. In the half-light, it seemed that even the pile of CDs on the floor knew they would not be seeing Robert again.

I had not done more than glance in the direction of the bedroom in the past. When I visited, the door would be open, but from my seat by the window, I could see only a bit of blank wall and the bathroom door beyond it. When I stepped into the room now, I discovered that his bed consisted of a single mattress lying on the floor. The sheets had been scattered in the general direction of the mattress rather than fitted to it, and a blanket spilled over them. A few books were stacked nearby.

I found the suitcase he had mentioned in the closet. It was more along the lines of a shopping cart than a suitcase, a cloth receptacle fitted over a metal frame attached to wheels. My seventy-nine-year-old mother had a similar conveyance, which she loved because it was so lightweight. I perused the clothes hanging in the closet: five pairs of pants (two corduroys and three chinos), five cotton button-down shirts, three flannel button-down shirts, and a plaid bathrobe. At the far end of the rack, I spotted the shirt with the Nehru collar Robert had worn to the ceremony at City Hall when he was named poet laureate. The flannel shirts looked worn, but the others had a distinctly new appearance. On closer examination, I saw the Lands' End and L.L. Bean labels. Once again, I realized how little I had thought about Robert's existence. I had never wondered how he came by his clothes and was surprised, though I shouldn't have been, to discover he was ordering them through the mail.

I took one pair of corduroy pants and one pair of chinos and set them in the bottom of the cart. I selected a mix of shirts and added them before going to the dresser. The top drawer of the dresser was filled with briefs neatly stacked in three piles. Most of them were white, with the Lands' End labels staring up at me, but a couple of pairs sported multicolored stripes. I selected a pile of the white briefs and placed them in the cart, feeling like an unwilling voyeur.

In the next drawer I found socks and, in the one below it, a couple of folded cardigan sweaters. I added a sweater, though he hadn't requested it, and discovered the slippers in the living room by his chair, along with the check and the bank deposit slip on the desk. The "very large" amount on the check was a hundred and eighty-seven dollars. I left everything else as I had found it, rolled the cart out into the hallway, and locked the door behind me. In the lobby I ran into the young man who lived down the hall with his cocker spaniel on a leash.

"You're Robert's friend, right?" he asked.

I nodded.

"Is he all right?"

"He's at Edgewood. I'm taking some of his things to him."

"I was afraid of this. He's been smoking again."

We exchanged looks, eyebrows raised, as if to say *what can you do?*

"Tell him I say hello," he said. "We miss him."

I told him I would convey the message and dragged the cart out into the night.

* * *

Robert sat in the chair wrapped in the flimsy robe supplied by the nursing home, the blue socks still adorning his feet. He watched as I took the underwear and socks from the wheeled cart and set them in a drawer marked with his name on a piece of masking tape. "I brought you a sweater," I said.

"I don't think I'll be needing that. It's far too hot."

I set the sweater in the drawer beside his underwear anyway. "I'll just put this in the closet," I said, indicating the wheeled cart.

He nodded.

The extra chair that had been available the last time I visited was gone, so I perched on the edge of the bed. The room was cramped and, indeed, overheated. His roommate lay in bed asleep as usual. Robert was so clearly in better shape than his roommate and the other patients who lined the halls. Even if he was dying, he was not in a zombie-like state. I felt keenly how wrong it was to find him in their midst.

"That was an errand of mercy," Robert said, inclining his head in the direction of the dresser. "Thank you."

We were both, I sensed, relieved to have gotten past the unpacking of the clothes.

"I've made some progress here," he said, spreading his thin fingers over his lap. "I've persuaded them to allow me a glass of wine with dinner. The doctor said he didn't think it could hurt. He's written a prescription. Six ounces a day. That makes things a bit more bearable." He smiled, clearly pleased with himself.

"Do they supply the wine?"

"Oh, no. Richard does. He brings me a delivery. In fact, he's been quite diligent about it. I'm afraid I'm a bit well stocked." He gestured toward the floor, where three unopened bottles sat beside his chair.

"Does he come every day?" I asked.

"Yes. His mother is here, down the hall. He stops in after he's visited her. I get snacks, too." Robert opened the drawer in the bedside table to reveal boxes of crackers and cookies, and some Power Bars. I could not quite see him eating Power Bars.

I had wondered how he obtained the wine he had offered me at his apartment. Now I knew.

As if on cue, a young woman in a nurse's uniform entered the room with a plastic cup in her hand. "Here's your wine, Mr. Dunn. Dinner will be in shortly."

"Could you bring a glass for my guest?" he said.

She responded quickly and firmly. "I can't serve wine to your guest. Just to you."

"Ah, I see," Robert said. "Doctor's orders."

The nurse smiled, seemingly in spite of herself. "Yes, doctor's orders."

When she was gone, I asked Robert about the food.

"It's not bad. Rather institutional, but not bad. They're going on about my weight again. They're quite obsessed about it, in fact. They want me to get up to a hundred pounds."

"Does that seem possible?"

"I'm at eighty-seven now. It seems like a tall order. Or perhaps that should be a fat order."

"Have you lost weight?"

He shrugged. "I don't think so. This is about where I've been for a while. I've never been particularly interested in food."

We talked for a while longer, and then I rose to go. "Is there anything else you need?"

"It will be quite nice to wear regular clothes," he said. "I'm quite set, thanks to you. Oh, but I could use a notebook. And a pen."

This, too, should have occurred to me. He needed his writing utensils. A few times in recent months Robert had mentioned that he was working on new poems. I had not imagined him writing here in the nursing home, but, as usual, he was focused on making the most of the present, while I was thinking only of the future.

* * *

Over the next couple of weeks, I visited every few days. Robert was still unable to walk and had to use the bedpan or commode. He was on oxygen all the time. We seemed to be in a holding pattern, waiting for what came next.

One afternoon he said, "I've been working on a poem. I wondered if you'd tell me what you think. I'm afraid my judgment may be a little off these days. I've been working on it for a couple of months now, and I think perhaps it's about there, but I'm not entirely sure."

He opened the notebook I had brought for him earlier that week and slid it toward me. I stared at the words neatly lined on the page as though encountering a foreign language. He had never shown me work in progress or asked for my assessment of his poems. Robert, it went without saying, did not need feedback. The typical writing workshop would have been anathema to him. I felt anxious about coming up with a response. Sharing drafts and giving each other criticism is standard in my friendships with a number of writers, but though I had talked *about* writing with Robert, any discussion of the work itself, his or mine, had remained off limits. That he wanted my opinion was a great tribute that made me just a bit nervous.

I read the poem through while he sat forward in his chair, his fingers pressed together. Like most of his poems, it was short and deceptively simple. I thought I had the gist of it on one reading, though later I would doubt I had grasped the poem at all. I read it through twice, aware of his eyes on me, but no matter how alertly he sat there, I could not convince myself that he truly cared about my opinion. No one could influence Robert. He was guided by nothing but his own sure voice.

The only criticism I could make would ask the poem to be something else—more expansive, maybe, or more explicit, but if the poem had done either of these things, it would not have been Robert's.

"It's wonderful," I said. "I can't see anything that should be changed. It feels finished."

"I'm afraid it's too poetic," he said. "This is something I always have to fight. One doesn't want to become too precious. In my current state, it's a bit harder to fight."

"I don't think it's too poetic," I said.

He gazed at me, as though waiting for more. He was serious, I saw, about wanting feedback. "Maybe it's done, but one can never be sure," he said. "I'm afraid I'm in a hurry, and that may cloud my vision."

"When you say you've been working on this for a couple of months, what do you mean?"

"Oh, I write them in my head," he said with a wave of his hand, as if to say the answer was obvious and not of much interest.

"In your head?" I echoed.

"Yes. I carry a poem around with me for two or three months."

"You don't write it down?"

"No. Not until I feel it's done. If it doesn't sound right when I say it over in my mind, I haven't gotten it yet. I keep working on it."

"You're not afraid you'll forget it?"

"Oh, no. Anything I need to remember, I'll remember. If it's good—or necessary—I won't forget it."

I thought of all the times I had seen Robert on the street and, in the early years, how he would look away, pretending he had not noticed me. I suppose I had always known that he must be writing poems in some fashion as he made his slow way to the center of town and back, but I had not stopped to think about it as I did now. That the poems were composed without even a typewriter or pen and paper, let alone a computer, made sense. They had the feel of something conjured from the air, distilled and refined by a process more elevated than the common rounds of drafts other writers engaged in.

I understood, in that moment, how completely Robert lived an interior life that was shaped by an almost ceaseless devotion to the word. I understood, too, how much he had lost when he could no longer walk. His method of composing was gone.

On an ordinary morning
The birds set out to find their King:
Thirty, all told, so few, so small
but a great longing was upon them.

All would have gone
but the thrush could not leave
her covert or the heron his marsh
or the eagle, alas, his coin.
last of all the gull
turned away with a despairing cry.

Night falls again, stars rise—
stars that are yes to the no of the night.
sometimes the yes is so little
it sounds like a no, but only the vulgar
spirited think it so.

—Robert Dunn

This is the poem Robert showed me that day at Edgewood. I found it, typed and unchanged, among his papers.

14.

Some Things Remain Unbroken

"I want to go home," Robert said to me one day shortly after I arrived to visit.

I tried to conceal my surprise. "What does the doctor say?"

"I haven't seen him in a week." He delivered this information in a tone of derision and annoyance. I should have known, he seemed to be saying, that the doctor was absent, though this was the first time he had given so much as a hint of being dissatisfied with the care he was receiving.

I sat perched on the edge of the bed while he remained in the chair, the little television dangling beside his head. Unable to compose myself quickly enough, I must have shown my apprehension. Robert leaned forward, his boney shoulders thrust toward me in a new attitude of defiance.

"There is no reason for me to stay here," he said.

I told him I would talk to the social worker.

He softened a bit after I made this offer, and we moved on to our ordinary round of topics, but the tension between us remained.

When I called the social worker, she said, "We don't think he can live on his own. He can't put on a pair of pants without help."

This struck me as definitive. How could he possibly return to his apartment if he could not even dress himself?

She added, "He can't take more than a few steps, and that's with a walker. The doctor won't give orders for him to be released."

I went to the nursing home a couple of days later and found Robert in no mood to talk about the weather or our mutual friends. "I am not staying here," he said. "If you will not agree to drive me home, I'll call a taxi."

I sat beside him in stunned silence. Hadn't we both, with deliberate grace, been preparing for his death? Apparently not. After a long moment, I said, "I spoke to the social worker. She says the doctor doesn't think you can manage on your own."

"I'm not staying here," he repeated. "Using that commode is just plain gross. Go to the drugstore and get me one of those deluxe walkers, the one with the seat on it. If I have that, I'll be fine."

The clipped words were a command, not a request. He had never spoken to me like this before. I could not see how he could return to his apartment in the shape he was in now, and I was not about to go purchase a walker. Breaking him out of the nursing home would remain his fantasy, not mine. When the aide arrived with his dinner, I said good-bye and made my way out of the cramped room.

* * *

A few years before Robert became sick, I began receiving news of friends and family members diagnosed with cancer on an almost monthly basis. The prayer list became a constant. When some went off the list, others took their places. In the space of four years, I lost seven close friends and family members, all of them but my ninety-two-year-old aunt to cancer. The rest went in their forties, fifties, and sixties, and two of the deaths, in my cousin's family, were children stricken with brain tumors. Any pretense that I might know how to respond to the approach of death, might be good at comforting myself or others, was taken from me. I would never be ready for this, never have the right words.

When Robert was transferred from the hospital to Edgewood, I was still trying to manage the situation with a sort of emotional efficiency. He quickly ripped this script from my hands. Death could not be pigeonholed, and neither could he. Carefully chosen words and actions were useless, even ridiculous. We were in messy, uncharted territory. He would not make it easy or predictable, and when he caught me trying to do so, he all but cringed. It was as if he was saying, "Don't make it pretty." I came to understand that the false effort to gloss over the nearness of death, to package its arrival into something that could be met with a resolute face, was something he would resist.

In retrospect, it is clear that several conversations should have taken place between me and Robert. We should have discussed how he envisioned these final stages of his life, and what I could do, and what I could not do, but at each new turn in this twisted road, I took my cue from him, and he did not initiate such conversation. Both of us were practiced at the art of indirection. Why should we adopt new strategies for communicating now? Robert chose me to be closely involved because, perhaps, he knew I would not force him into the sort of emotional processing he hated, but my reticence, with which Robert was comfortable, made me less than ideal, it would become clear, to handle this increasingly complex situation.

* * *

The morning after my visit the social worker called to inform me a meeting had been scheduled for the next day to discuss Robert's situation. He had requested I be present. I could not imagine facing this alone and recruited Mimi to come with me. When we arrived, we found Robert's sister, a man I took to be her husband, and Robert's brother already crowded into the room. His brother sat in a wheelchair, a canister of oxygen propped between his legs. Like Robert, he had COPD. I was not aware, until I entered the room that morning, of his existence.

The presence of these family members seemed to be as great a surprise to Robert as it was to me. The social worker and a hospice representative sat pressed together on the bed. Mimi and I squeezed in beside them. The social worker began by thanking us for coming and said, "We're all here because we want what's best for Robert."

"Then you will let me go home," Robert said.

"It will have to be against doctor's orders," the hospice person said. "The doctor won't give approval for you to go home." She spoke slowly and quietly, as though addressing a child.

Robert's eyes flashed. "I don't need the doctor's approval."

There was a long silence in which we all looked at each other, uncertain how to proceed.

"The doctor does not feel you can manage on your own," the social worker said.

"That's not his decision to make," Robert said. "I'll call a taxi if I have to."

"We understand that you'd like to be at home," the hospice woman said. "But what would you have at home that you don't have here? Maybe we can make you more comfortable here."

"You see, I want to write," he said, and now Robert was the one to adopt the tone of a parent lecturing a child. "It is almost impossible for me to write here. Without poetry, I do not see that life is worth living."

"We could consider sending you home with hospice care, but we can only do that if there is someone else living with you in your apartment," the woman from hospice said. "There has to be a caretaker in the home. Is that a possibility?"

Robert responded promptly, "No, I don't want that."

"Then the only choice is to go home against doctor's orders," she said.

Robert's sister interrupted. "You can come and live with me."

Robert gave her a withering look. "I don't think either of us wants to consider that option."

Another silence ensued as we all seemed to be wondering whether any other course of action remained. Robert's brother shifted in his chair and said quietly, "I love you, buddy."

Robert responded with a nod in his direction.

The social worker turned to me. "Do you think Robert's friends in town could give him enough help if he goes home?"

I did not want to answer this question because it was clear, with the eyes of everyone in the room on me, that I had to say yes.

I glanced at Mimi. "I think we could," I said.

Mimi nodded in assent. "There are quite a few of us. We could set up a schedule."

The man I took to be Robert's brother-in-law spoke for the first time (later Robert would explain that he and Robert's sister were not married). "You people are crazy. He could live another six months. You have no idea what you're talking about. You have no idea how much care he's going to need. You're nuts."

As I tried to take in his dismissive tone and angry look, I saw that Robert's sister was crying. She waved one hand in the air and said, "His poetry friends were always more important."

The scene was quickly devolving into a bad drama, one scripted by Robert, with roles assigned to each of us without our consent. Mimi put her hand on my arm and whispered, "Let's go."

Mimi stood and addressed the circle of faces ringing the room. "We're going to leave now. We think it would be best if Robert and his family worked out the details on their own."

"You're his family," Robert's sister said accusingly as we moved toward the door.

"No," Mimi said, "you are."

We reached the hallway and walked quickly to the main entrance, arms linked, both of us pushing back tears. I felt a terrific sadness, and anger, that Robert could not accept the help everyone in that room was trying to give, that it must be his way or no way. His sister, it appeared, wanted to take care of him, or was at least willing to do so, but he had rejected this possibility with complete disdain. That he used his poetry to justify his rejection of her offer and all other options struck me as self-centered and heartless. The tears were for both of us, me and Robert, and how impossible the situation had become.

* * *

There have been many times I have considered giving up writing, when the thread of an uneasy belief in my work snaps. No one is asking me to do this thing, which sometimes feels too hard and doesn't pay a living wage. Does the world need another book? In my low moments, it is difficult to make this argument.

Each time I am ready to give up, I hear a voice in my head—my own stubborn one—saying, *You can't stop writing.* I know that without writing I turn into a dried husk of myself. There's no ground beneath me at all if I'm not writing.

Robert's declaration to all of us gathered in his room at the nursing home was one I had made myself. *I can't live without writing.* But on that day and under those circumstances, I saw him as being willfully controlling. As much as I empathized with his wishes, I did not think he had the luxury of putting the writing before all else, not at the stage he had reached now. My reaction revealed the fault line in my understanding of both Robert and myself. The writing might be more important to us than anything else, but could we insist that others see it that way, too?

There's no denying gender here. As a woman, I have a hard time claiming time for myself. Putting the writing first? That's even harder. I have not been able to kill the angel in the house, as Virginia Woolf said women who are writers must. I have become good at fitting the writing in around laundry and cooking and cleaning; around earning a living, and taking vacations with my husband, and visiting my family. Robert had never needed to make such concessions. As a man was he freer to shrug off those expectations? No doubt this was a piece of it, though he had always seemed to transcend gender and so much else. He existed outside these definitions entirely. How often I had admired his pure devotion to poetry and his refusal to conform, but in the waning days of that year, his choices looked different to me.

* * *

The day after the meeting at the nursing home, the social worker called. "I just want to update you on Robert," she said.

I leapt to the conclusion that she was calling with grave news. She was, but not of the sort I imagined.

"After the meeting yesterday we explained to him that if he goes home against doctor's orders, he won't be able to get the services he's had—the visiting nurses and aides. He became very despondent. He's disconnected his oxygen."

Before I could say anything, she went on. "He can't kill himself doing this. He thinks he'll die without the oxygen. But he won't. He'll just make himself very uncomfortable."

"So he's just sitting there without the oxygen?"

"Yes. He said he'd rather die than stay here. We've explained to him he's not going to kill himself this way."

"And he hasn't reconnected the oxygen?"

"No."

I thanked her for letting me know and said I would come over.

I finished an editing job I was working on and drove to the nursing home. On my way to Robert's room, I stopped at the nurses' station. They told me that he had reconnected the oxygen shortly after the social worker called me.

He was seated in the chair by the bed with the oxygen tubes protruding from his nostrils, staring at the wall. His arms lay rigidly in his lap. He rotated his head when I said his name and gazed at me blankly.

"Are you all right?" I asked.

He nodded the barest hint of a response.

"Are you in pain?"

He stared at me for a long moment before answering, his voice a hoarse whisper, "Not any more than usual."

I reached into the canvas bag I had brought with me. "I have some more books for you."

He gave the books a cursory glance as I set them on the table by the bed, instead of examining each one in turn as he usually did.

"Jim thought you might like this one." I indicated a memoir on top of the stack.

He extended his neck ever so slightly in acknowledgment.

I attempted to fill the strained space between us. I told him I had heard from a couple of friends who were planning to come and visit. He acknowledged each of my statements with nothing more than a glance in my general direction. After fifteen minutes of this one-sided exchange, I rose to go.

Robert may have been despondent, but he was also angry, and I saw that anger as directed at me now. As I threaded through the overheated corridors of the nursing home, my own anger filled me like the buzzing of the fluorescent lights overhead. His suicide attempt, if it could be called that, struck me, like the scene the day before, as a melodramatic act smacking of a misplaced narcissism. At every turn, he had blocked any attempt at a workable solution to his situation. He would continue to live, so long as he remained in this world, on his own terms, no matter what this imposed on others.

The social worker called the next morning to tell me they were trying to put together a plan to send Robert home before Christmas, even if it meant releasing him against doctor's orders. She called later in the day with the news that Robert was having panic attacks again. Until the panic attacks were under control, the plan to send him home was off. This was the first I had heard of panic attacks, but the way she spoke of them indicated it was not a new development. The words "panic" and "attack" in connection with Robert filled me with a confused dismay. I was certain for a moment I had heard her wrong. I would learn later that this is common in COPD patients who have to struggle simply to breathe, but on that day, the term *panic attack* echoed in my mind after I hung up the phone, a reflection of how low Robert and I had both sunk.

I was seated at my desk writing the following morning when the phone rang again. I saw on the caller ID that it was the nursing home and picked up. The social worker told me that Robert had been diagnosed with pneumonia. There was no question of his going home now. We did not speak of his suicide attempt or the panic attacks again.

* * *

I assumed, like the nurses and doctors, that the pneumonia signaled the end. Recovery from the collapsed lung, and now this, did not seem possible. If Robert had pneumonia, we would no longer be discussing sending him home, or how his other friends and I could care for him. I was relieved to have my sense of responsibility for Robert lifted, to focus on decorating the Christmas tree and taking boxes of gifts to the post office. I longed for what was concrete and simple, and Christmas, which usually had its share of tense moments, suddenly seemed easy.

My mother arrived a few days before the holiday. I did not go to visit Robert again until the day before New Year's, when the house was empty of guests and quiet again. He was in a single room now, around the corner from his old room. I knew that he had moved, but had not seen the new room yet. I cautiously knocked on the shut door and heard the low murmur of his "come in." The open space of the large room struck me immediately as less institutional than the previous one. Here he would have the privacy that he wanted. Through the double windows, there was a view of a courtyard, an improvement over his old view of the parking lot.

He was seated in a chair with an open book in his lap. I took the chair beside his, reminded of our times at his apartment.

"What a nice room," I said.

Robert nodded. "Yes, they've been most accommodating."

"How are you feeling?"

"Quite a bit better. The pneumonia has cleared up."

"Really?" I said, unable to cover my surprise. "That's wonderful. So what does the doctor say about your lungs?"

"They're back to normal. Or what passes for normal in my case."

"That's wonderful," I repeated.

"I'm ready to go home."

"Is that what the doctor says?"

"No. He won't give orders for me to go home."

I tried to think quickly of a response that would not inflame him. "That makes it kind of challenging."

"If you won't get me out of here, I'll find someone who will," he said. "You're trying to warehouse me in this place."

I was so shocked by this, I could not speak. I could not have imagined, before this moment, a circumstance in which I would be accused of trying to "warehouse" anyone anywhere. I felt angry and betrayed, cut to the core. After all I had done, how could he make such an accusation?

"Do you feel you're not getting adequate care?" I said finally.

"No, the care is more than adequate."

"They arranged for you to have this single room."

"Yes, that was quite good of them. Everyone at Edgewood has done their best to make me comfortable. That is not the issue. I won't stay here. You might like to see what Marie has done." He produced a piece of paper from the inside cover of his book and handed it to me.

I saw, after a quick glance, that it was a letter addressed to his doctor. Marie, a local writer, was one of those who had known Robert since the 1970s. She had asked me for updates when I ran into her at the monthly poetry readings, but she had not, to my knowledge, been to visit Robert, though now I discovered that she had been to the nursing home on at least one occasion, when according to the letter, she and the doctor had met. The letter continued:

First, I think you need to know that Robert Dunn, Portsmouth's second Poet Laureate, is a writer of great accomplishment and a man who has advanced the cause of poets and poetry all his life. He is also a man who has lived a very simple, not to say ascetic life, eschewing most of the things of this world in favor of the pursuit of art and service to his fellow humans. He has virtually no money as far as I know. If he were living in Europe or Scandinavia, his last months, weeks and days might be spent in some sort of "assisted living" situation. But he lives in

America, and we don't provide most of our citizens this kind of end of life care.

Now Robert is gravely ill. He may be dying. He's perfectly aware of that. But perhaps not yet (he's demonstrated an amazing resilience over and over). What is clear, though, is that he does not want extraordinary measures taken to keep him alive, nor does he wish to die in a hospital or nursing home except as a last resort. He does, however, want to continue writing what he knows may be his best poems.

If you refuse to discharge him from Edgewood once this pneumonia has been beaten back with antibiotics, Robert will, I'm certain, insist on leaving anyway. This will mean he will have no medical/home services, scant and inadequate as those services are. If, on the other hand, you agree that he may be discharged to his home, he will enjoy the few services he's entitled to, and he will have the daily ministrations of a phalanx of friends who have committed to visiting and tending to his basic needs. When you think about it, no social service or assisted living situation could be better than that from the viewpoint of the person on the receiving end.

The letter ended with a "respectful suggestion" that the doctor consider Robert's wishes.

Robert's eyes were trained on me when I looked up. So this was what he wanted, a crusader, a champion for his cause. Fine, I thought, he had found one. Marie could write all the letters she liked. She would not be the one to get the phone calls if he returned home.

I could barely take in the words on the page in my shaking hand. Later Marie would give me a copy of the letter, and I would see that her tone was reasonable, but at that moment it struck me as an indictment of what I had not done. Tense with rage, I handed the letter to Robert.

To be blamed for not making his wishes possible was ridiculous. I was determined to walk out of the room without saying another word. Robert had crossed a line that I was not willing to cross with him. He had placed me in the position of acting truly as a family member and forced a responsibility on me that it seemed I had not accepted or agreed to, except that in the halting steps that led to this day, I had. I was as angry at myself over this as I was at him, but one thing was glaringly clear. I was not going to take on responsibility for the situation now, not if he was this ungrateful.

Before I could make my exit, a knock sounded on the door. I expected one of the friendly aides, but Pat and Manny stepped into the room. Robert greeted them with his usual dignified cordiality, all traces of our exchange vanished.

Pat and her husband, Manny, were not among those who had visited Robert regularly, but they knew him, like so many others did, from the Poetry Hoot and the streets of Portsmouth. The week before, they had sent me a beautiful bouquet of Christmas flowers with a card thanking me for caring for Robert. I was ready to rush into the safe and neutral ground of their arms.

They asked Robert how he was doing and asked about my Christmas with my mother. They told us about visits from their children. We passed ten minutes in ordinary conversation, with Robert playing host, before I made my exit. Once out of the room, I threaded through the corridors to the main entrance barely able to see what was in front of me, still reeling from the blow he had delivered as surely as a left hook to the jaw.

A week later, the social worker called to tell me that Robert was going to be discharged under the doctor's orders. I had not been back to visit or called him.

"We've arranged for a hospital bed to be delivered to his apartment," the social worker said. "He'll have a deluxe walker and an oxygen machine. He will need to be on oxygen most of the time. With all this in place, the doctor is willing to sign the order."

"How is he going to get home?" I asked.

"By ambulance. The EMTs will come and transport him. But someone needs to be at his apartment when he arrives. We can't release him otherwise. Do you think you could be there? We're planning on Wednesday morning."

"I'm trying to be less involved."

"So you can't be there?"

"No, I can't."

"Is there anyone else?"

"I'll see if I can find someone."

I hung up the phone and sent an email to the collection of Poet Laureate Program board members who received my regular updates on Robert's condition. Liz said she could be at the apartment. I spent the morning when he returned home at my desk working on the next novel.

* * *

The handmade book was tiny, about two inches square, with marbled paper on the cover and a black binding. I opened it to find "for Katie" written in black ink on the inside front cover. Each of the book's five pages contained a single, handwritten word on the front and back. Together they read: "Even so some things remain unbroken. Any stone however small is whole." The inside back cover bore the signature "Yrs. Robert."

He sat in the chair opposite me, his eyes attentive and bright behind the lenses of his glasses. "My friend Lynne made that little book," he said. "I thought you might like it."

"It's beautiful," I said. "I love the poem."

"Is it a poem? Ah, yes, I guess it is."

"What isn't a poem?"

He smiled. "I can think of a few things. George Bush, for one."

"No, he's not a poem, decidedly."

"Or he's a very bad one. There's a place, of course, for bad poetry, though I would put him in another category."

"Speaking of poems, have you been writing?" I said.

Robert brought his hands together in that meditative way of his. "I've done a bit. I'm afraid it takes a great deal of time to manage all the medications and entertain the visiting nurse and aide." He gestured toward the litter of medical supplies on his desk. "What about you? Have you been playing with poetry again?"

"I have a lot of drafts. Folders of them. But I don't seem to be in a poetry frame of mind. I take them out and look at them and put them back. They don't make sense to me. I don't know what they're about."

"Oh, Katie," Robert said, his voice laced with amused irritation. "Of course you don't. None of us know what our poems are about."

I reached for my teacup on the table between us, and we went on to other topics—if there was any hope for the upcoming presidential election, and how he was faring with his food deliveries. Meals on Wheels now came twice a day, another of the requirements imposed by the nursing home on his release.

This was my first visit since his return home several weeks earlier. I had stayed away, still stung by our encounter at the nursing home. I had received updates from Mimi and Liz and others who brought him books and soup. I fully expected that he would return to the hospital or nursing home any day, but once again Robert defied the odds. Mimi and Liz reported that he was doing quite well. I relented finally and called him, and he asked if I would come by for tea. This is how we resolved whatever there was to resolve, by simply resuming our old patterns.

I stayed for about forty-five minutes that day. He was not on oxygen, but I knew that he would loop the lines around his ears as soon as I left. Talking clearly tired him. I tried not to make him laugh, but it was hard to avoid with his quick repartee. As it had in the past, our conversation felt like a dance, a merry sort of jig, in which he was always a few steps ahead of me. There was pleasure in trying to keep up.

I finished my tea and said I would be going.

"I appreciate your stopping by," Robert said.

I nodded and slipped the little book he had given me into my pocket. I recognized the spare and carefully written words as an apology of sorts, the only acknowledgment I would receive of what had taken place between us.

* * *

We had a new narrative now, this one about recovery and survival. Robert was going on; in fact, he was doing far more than that. He was taking brief walks to the bank and bookstore. The deluxe walker made it possible for him to go half a block, sit down for a short rest, and move on. He had mastered carrying the small oxygen canister with him in a little backpack, so he could go out while on oxygen.

Three years had passed since Robert's first hospitalization, when he was still on Whidden Street and asked Connie to call the ambulance at one in the morning. Four months had passed since the social worker told me he had two or three weeks to live. Through this long, tangled time of weeks that turned into months, and months that turned into years, I often wished I had been given some instructions, a map for how this was supposed to proceed and what I was supposed to do, but a death from COPD, I learned, is among the most unpredictable. I gradually came to accept the fact that the doctors could not make any pronouncements about Robert's prognosis or possible future that would hold. He took great pleasure in proving them wrong.

As he continued to access an increasing number of support services, I visited every couple of weeks. My visits seldom overlapped with those of the nurses and aides who came regularly in the mornings. Robert and I talked, drank tea or wine, and traded books and magazines. I no longer thought of these days as his last. The timeline was gone, replaced by repeated rounds of dread and hope as Robert got worse and got better and got worse again.

After the confrontation in the nursing home, we were careful with each other, and the distance between us felt like a necessary correction. Robert made sure that what he needed could be taken care of by the visiting nurses and the home health aides. He did not call on me as he had in the past. It was as if we had broken up and gotten back together, which in a way we had. Our affection and admiration for each other remained, but it was muted, more tentative, now that we knew anger could break out between us. Robert had been disappointed in me for not living up to the role he had imagined me playing. He appeared resolved not to misjudge me again. I was resolved to be clear about just how much he could expect from me.

From the notebooks of Robert Dunn

Little gray birds
move just outside my window.
Turning painfully on a wounded side
I can just make them out. And no
I will not ring for morphine just yet.
This is a country torturers come from.
Tell me a land of honor and truth
yet lives, tell me.

15.

Historic District

The Music Hall, constructed in 1878, is tucked on a side street downtown. When Jim and I moved to Portsmouth, the old theater had just been saved from the wrecking ball by a group of citizens who formed a nonprofit to keep it going. We went to the Music Hall regularly to see independent and foreign films, despite the fact that in the winter the lack of heat meant wearing a coat for the duration of the movie. The worn seats had cratered hollows in their centers, and the red leather was almost entirely worn away. We had our own seats, as we thought of them, ones we had discovered in a row down front that were in a bit better condition than the rest. They were usually empty, even when we arrived minutes before the curtain, because the theater was seldom more than half-full. Ollie, a stray cat the staff had taken in when he showed up in the alley next to the theater, added to the feeling that we were watching movies in a run-down communal living room. Ollie's home was the green room backstage, but he usually woke up about halfway through the movie and came strolling across the stage, his profile stamped on the screen. He would descend the steps at the edge of the stage and wander through the rows of seats meowing until he found a suitable lap to jump into. Ollie never chose my lap, to my disappointment, but watching him make a tour of the theater was entertainment enough, sometimes better than the movie.

The Music Hall in its funky, dilapidated splendor perfectly represented the Portsmouth of the early 1990s—shabby and comfortable around the edges, unpretentious, and full of potential. Now that potential was being realized in spades. High-end restaurants and boutique food and clothing stores were moving into one storefront after another downtown like a collection of overdressed starlets. The interior of the Music Hall was in the process of being restored, the seats replaced and the ornate ceiling returned to its original glory. Ollie no longer strolled across the stage during movies, and the theater was almost always packed. A new program, Writers on a New England Stage, brought people like Margaret Atwood and Barbara Kingsolver to speak to sold-out crowds.

"We've been discovered—again," I said to Jim on more than one occasion, my tone a mix of pride and chagrin. Portsmouth was not our secret anymore. It seemed bad-spirited, bordering on petulant, to bemoan these changes. We could walk to a theater offering an incredible array of events and a gorgeous interior, but the new ticket prices were steep, and I missed Ollie.

I missed the Robert of our first years in Portsmouth, too. I longed to see him passing silently on the street in his old coat with its outdated dignity, someone I knew but did not quite know. The Robert of those days belonged to a time when he and I had still escaped definition, at least in relation to each other. Now both of us—and our town—seemed to have adopted personas that did not quite suit us. I was not the ideal caretaker, and he was not the ideal patient.

* * *

We had never run into Robert at the Music Hall. I assumed he did not attend movies, such a frivolous and extravagant pursuit being unnecessary to him, but with the acquisition of a television and DVD player, he could watch them in his apartment now. The television was a recent gift from Mimi, who had inherited the old set when her mother-in-law died.

"I was quite amazed by what they made out of the snowstorm on TV," Robert said when I visited his apartment one day. "A few inches of snow. You would have thought the end of the world was at hand."

Robert told me that other than movies he watched the news mostly and liked New England Cable News best. I was addicted to this station myself for its thorough and frequent weather reports. The broadcasters did go to extremes in covering the weather, but I was as caught up in the overblown drama as anyone else. I appreciated Robert's detached view of television, seeing through his eyes how real-time coverage warps our sense of the importance of events by providing no context for them. All we have is a continuous stream of screaming headlines.

Sometimes I struggled to find topics for conversation while Robert sat beside me with the oxygen line threaded over his ears and into his nose, his chest rising and falling in a heaving rhythm with each breath. Other visits our talk flew. I never knew what sort of day it would be until I took a seat beside him. His world had narrowed to his small apartment, what the TV brought him, and the dim corridors of his building, though he still occasionally ventured a few blocks with the walker.

The time I spent with Robert now was marked by moments shot through with urgency, and others that were full of a sweet slowness. Every visit, every poem, every phone call might be the last, and this awareness suffused our interactions with a heightened sensibility that was wonderful and exhausting. The words we spoke began to seem like jewels strung on a chain, each worth so much, and yet the daily grind of his illness with its repeated crises and recoveries thwarted any attempt to shape the story in a redemptive arc. Every conversation was both precious and ordinary, each new stage in the progression of Robert's illness unimaginable and mundane.

On just a couple of occasions he spoke briefly about how sick he was. One of these times I was complaining about some inconsequential thing in my life, as I had a tendency to do. He gave me an aggrieved look and said, "Imagine facing your own mortality."

The expression on his face was one of impatient pleading. I murmured some words of sympathy and waited for him to say more. We sat there for a long moment gazing at each other, and then he moved on to something else. How do you talk about death with someone who is dying? My chest clenched tight in fear. I was afraid of saying the wrong thing, revealing my complete insensitivity in taking life for granted as I could not help but do, being so firmly planted in the land of the living. At root, though, my fear was a muted terror I could barely acknowledge to myself, let alone anyone else, at the idea of death itself.

* * *

I came home from a business trip to find a message from Jim on the kitchen table. Scrawled on the back of a used envelope, it read: "Call Robert. At Edgewood."

I had been gone for five days. In that time, it appeared, Robert had been hospitalized and released to the nursing home.

He did not have a phone in his room yet, I assumed. Whether he would stay long enough this time to make arranging for a phone necessary remained to be seen. I called the nurses' station on his floor, a number I had memorized, and they carried a phone in to him.

His voice had an uncertain, wavering quality as he said hello.

"I've been away," I told him. "On a freelance project."

"Ah," he said. "I trust your travels went well."

A pause followed, in which neither of us spoke. He didn't volunteer to explain the current situation. "What's going on?" I asked finally.

"Oh, just more of the same. I'm afraid I had to go to the hospital the other night."

"You called the ambulance?"

"Yes. They've got me on a new medication. They want to keep me here at Edgewood a bit longer."

I questioned him about when exactly he went to the hospital. Saturday, he told me, the night before I left for my trip. Further prodding on my part established that he had been at Edgewood for three days. I asked if any visitors had been to see him, though what I was really trying to figure out, in the indirect way I had taken to adopting, was whether he had notified anyone.

"Liz called and didn't get an answer at my apartment. She was a bit worried, I take it. She tracked me down and came by yesterday. We had a good visit."

When he said nothing more, I asked, "Do you need anything?"

"Liz brought something of a collection of books. But I could use some clothes. I came away rather quickly."

I told him I would go by his apartment the next day and pick up some things for him.

When I let myself into the apartment, I found signs of a hasty departure. The line to the oxygen snaked in coiled circles across the floor. A half-full glass of orange juice sat on the table by the chair, a plate with a piece of toast smeared with congealed butter beside it. His table was covered in papers that looked like they had been blown there by a sudden wind. I looked for evidence of poems but found instead instructions for medications, a form having to do with his housing, and a booklet on managing COPD. I poured the orange juice down the drain, tossed the toast in the trash, and did the dishes.

The hospital bed was raised halfway, the sheets wadded at the foot of the mattress. I wondered if he slept sitting up now. I went through his drawers collecting underwear and socks. Liz had a key to the apartment, but he had not asked her to get his clothes and would not, I saw now, were the situation to recur. I was the only one who would be given this intimate task. Robert had managed for some time without directly asking for my help, but when pressed, when he could find no one else, he still turned to me. I accepted this now, and accepted that there might be more hospitalizations and phone calls, more trips to his apartment and back to Edgewood.

This reality was brought home to me when I arrived at Edgewood and discovered Robert sitting in the chair by the bed in a skimpy johnny and robe. His face brightened as I entered the room.

"I was getting a bit tired of wearing these digs," he said as I hung a couple of button-down shirts from hooks in the cabinet across from his bed.

I felt reproached and helpless. For four days he had been sitting there in that johnny waiting for me.

I understood, more clearly than I had before, that I was the one Robert would allow to see his full vulnerability. If I, and no one else, retrieved clothes from his apartment and learned of his panic attacks from the social worker, he could continue to be the Penny Poet of Portsmouth. He could go on entertaining his guests with his witty observations and references to obscure poets, freed of the need to discuss his health or how he was managing. He could hang on to an appearance of autonomy.

Robert's somewhat tenuous life in Portsmouth had rested on his complete independence. He had always been free to define his time as he wanted, other than the few hours he put in at the Athenaeum.

No one had the right, or any reason, to ask him to meet their expectations. He conformed to no ideas but his own.

Robert took great pride in his independence. Now in a multitude of ways he had lost that independence. He relied on an array of social services and a collection of people like me who visited him. Without all of us his existence would have been impossible. Still, I saw, he needed to believe in the independence that had defined him for so long. If I was the only one who went through his sock drawer, it would be easier for him to preserve this belief.

Something simpler was no doubt also going on. He hated asking for help. He had become accustomed, as much as he disliked it, to asking me. If he wasn't exactly comfortable relying on me, he was used to it by now. As one friend said, when I wondered aloud why Robert had chosen me to run these errands, "You were there."

* * *

Robert stayed at Edgewood just a week that time. His condition once again stabilized. I assumed he was not smoking, which accounted at least in part for the latest comeback.

One day when he was back in his apartment and I came to visit, he said, "I have something for you."

He handed me a copy of his new chapbook. Titled *Je ne regrette rien* after the Édith Piaf song, it was published by Oyster River Press out of Durham, New Hampshire. Oyster River had brought out a collection of Robert's poems titled *I Hear America Singing* in 2006 as part of their *Walking to Windward* series of books by New England poets. The earlier, full-length book contained some new work with poems that Robert had published previously in his penny collections and *quo, Musa, tendis?* The title for the series of all twenty books (*Walking to Windward*) was a line from one of Robert's poems, and his book was the first published in the series. *Je ne regrette rien* again collected older work with a couple of new poems, in a beautiful little pocket-sized edition.

"Can I pay you for this?" I said after I had remarked on how handsome the book was.

"No, no. I have plenty of copies. More than I know what to do with, I fear."

"Will you sign it then?"

He reached for a pen on the table and wrote on the inside cover: "For Katie on the first summer's day. Not to be compared except with fondness—Robert"

"And how is your writing coming?" he asked.

We were seated in our accustomed places, with the teapot on the table, our teacups and the plate of butter cookies beside it.

"I wrote most of a new chapter last week, but I'm having a hard time figuring out the points of view," I said. "I keep going back and forth."

Robert nodded. "No doubt that's what you need to do."

"No doubt. But it's driving me crazy."

"Ah, yes, trying to find the right words will do that to you."

We sat in silence for a moment, and I reached for my teacup.

"I hope I will get to read this book," he said. "I want to see how it all turns out."

I met his gaze. His look was devoid of emotion, but I understood what he was saying.

The next morning I went to my desk with a renewed sense of purpose. Robert was waiting, and he didn't have much time. A few weeks later, I printed out what I had written so far, the first one hundred fifty pages of the manuscript. There were a few gaps I had yet to fill in, but most of the pages were coherent enough, if not anything close to finished. It felt like handing over a naked doll whose wardrobe I was still designing. I had shown a few chapters to a couple of readers, but no one else had read beyond that. Robert would be my first reader, a fact about which I had some trepidation. I did not expect him to be the most gentle or forgiving critic.

Some months earlier, I had told Robert about meeting with a book group that had read my first novel. "They complained about the sad ending," I said. "I've gotten a lot of that. It never even occurred to me how people would react when I was writing it. It simply seemed like what had to happen."

"Then it was what had to happen, no doubt. What would your readers have preferred? For Alice and Pete to settle down and raise a brood of kids?"

"I guess." This was the first time he had referred to my book in anything but the most general terms. I was touched to discover that he was familiar enough with the characters to mention them by name.

Robert gave a short laugh at my response. "That wouldn't make for much of an ending."

"No, but people seem to be very attached to Pete."

"I thought he was a bit too perfect myself." He made this comment in his usual muted tone, without elaborating. It was a small comment, slipped in before we moved on to something else, but I did not forget it. His pronouncement had the sting of truth. I had created a character who was not complex enough, and in his non-confrontational, understated way, Robert had pointed this out to me.

The moment was the sort that writers will do anything to avoid. I found the questions from the book groups by turns puzzling and annoying, but I could return to the four walls of my office at home and dismiss them. Robert's comment went to the heart of what mattered to me most. His quick observation had stayed with me as I worked on my third book. Now I waited nervously for his feedback.

He took his time reading the pages, but in September a letter arrived.

Portsmouth, NH
September 17, 2007

Dear Katie,

I've enjoyed the chance to see volume three under construction. So perhaps a few observations from a sidewalk superintendent would be in order.

The first chapter introduces Liza and the reader to the island in an easy and natural way. It was pleasant to encounter Alice and the store and much else as the story advances—even George Tibbits, which was a bit of a surprise. And no doubt they provide the new reader with background, depth, distant vistas and suchlike.

The changing point of view seems to work. Allows you to get in stuff that would be awkward to include otherwise. The first transition from Ruth to Nick is something of a speed bump. Perhaps you could find a way to ease the transition. For example, the last sentence of the first chapter might have a reference to geese to be echoed in the first sentence of the second. A bit artificial no doubt, but I'm sure the geese are very important. At least geese always seem to think so.

I notice that Alice's braid is white on one page and gray on another. All in the eyes of the beholder of course. I imagine that Lydia's hair, if it appears, will be blue.

It's interesting to see two generations dealing with the same kind of relationship in Nora and Ruth. I find myself wishing that at least one of the lesbian couples will be together at the end of the story. (An attack of family values no doubt.)

Actually the blanks in the manuscript are kind of appeal-ing to the imagination: "You-know-who has been feeding the geese again." When you come to think of it there's really no reason that everyone should have a name. Granted that it's convenient for many purposes, but remembering names is such a bother.

I did enjoy looking over the shoulder of a photographer at work. Something one never gets to do in daily life—although you must have done it somehow. Always a pleasure to be with people who are doing or thinking interesting things, if only in a book.

Even people who are tedious in our common lives might be interesting in a story. Is there any chance of the Robin-son family conducting human sacrifices at the time of the full moon? That old-time religion, you know.

Cheers,
Robert

The Robinsons, whose name got changed in later drafts, are the island's fundamentalist Christians—"tedious" in real life but "inter-esting" in a story, according to Robert.

The sly humor of Robert's letter was endearing, but like most writers, anything less than a Nobel Prize is not enough praise for me. Did he actually like the book? I couldn't tell. The complete dispas-sion of his response was refreshing in its way. He was able to stand back from it in a fashion I was not, and that in itself was helpful. He pointed out something I had not noticed, that two of the major relationships in the book were headed for potential heartbreak. His comment about this influenced me in later drafts.

I wasn't expecting enthusiastic encouragement from Robert, and I didn't get it, but knowing that he had read the manuscript and gotten something of the book's spirit, as his response seemed to reveal, was enough.

* * *

As everyone in New Hampshire did, we talked a great deal about politics that fall. Say what you will about the first in the nation primary—and there is plenty to criticize—New Hampshire voters take the responsibility seriously. In the lead-up to the 2008 primary, most Democrats I know made it a point to see every candidate in person, and many agonized over the decision until they walked into the voting booth.

"I don't think it much matters who I might vote for," Robert said one afternoon. "I don't think I'll be here for the primary."

"I don't know about that," I said. The primary was only a few months away. "I would think it over if I were you."

"I can't say I'm terribly enthused about any of them, except Kucinich."

I had met Kucinich at a house party when he ran in 2004. "He stayed for about ten minutes and then had to go because he was doing a TV taping in Manchester," I told Robert. "It was about zero degrees out, and when they went out to the car, the locks had frozen. So he came back inside and said, 'I'd much rather be here than doing a TV interview.' He was very real, very approachable. But he can't get elected. It's too important this time. I want to vote for someone who has a chance."

"I voted for Nader in 2000," Robert said.

I tried, without much success, to hide my chagrin, though I recognized this act as consistent with Robert's stubborn principles.

"Nader handed Bush the election," I said. "Well, the Supreme Court handed Bush the election, but if it hadn't been for Nader, New Hampshire would have gone to Gore, and the whole mess in Florida wouldn't have mattered."

Robert nodded his assent to this assessment, though his expression did not convey any regret. When he didn't say more, I added, "I hope to God Nader doesn't run this time."

As I drove home that night, I thought of all the principled left-wingers, like Robert, who had voted for Nader, and the consequences of those votes. I knew all the arguments. We're in thrall to the two-party system, and that system is bankrupt; the Democrats and Republicans are bought and sold by the corporations; change will only come if enough people stand up for it. In theory, I agreed with these arguments, but there was too much at stake in 2000, far more than we could know at the time.

I watched all the debates in the weeks that followed, read the editorials, and thought about almost nothing else. A friend in New York who is a Democratic organizer called to urge me to vote for Chris Dodd. Friends in Ohio lobbied for Hillary Clinton. In early December, when I saw Barack Obama speak in the gym of the Exeter high school, I made my decision. He was inspiring, electrifying, smart, and genuine—the whole package. No one I had ever voted for in the New Hampshire primary had gone all the way to the White House. I hoped this time would be different.

* * *

In November, Robert gave a reading from his new chapbook at RiverRun Bookstore. He asked two local poets to read with him, but Robert was the star that Sunday afternoon, and everyone knew it. He sat on the little seat of his walker and spoke into a microphone, more audibly than I could remember ever hearing him. Each word came through with a bell-like clarity. He recited the poems from memory, his face turned toward the ceiling, and then signed books for the crowd gathered around the table. He made it through the reading without oxygen but attached the lines to the portable canister afterward. He glowed with pride and his mischievous brand of happiness as he greeted the throng gathered around him.

The week before Christmas I went to City Hall and got an application for an absentee ballot. After much drama and machinations, the date of the primary had finally been set, and it would fall right after New Year's. Robert had made it to the bookstore for his reading, but he said that going to the polls would be too difficult and offered this as a reason not to vote. I countered with the absentee ballot application, which I delivered with a jar of jelly and a Christmas card. Another Christmas, and Robert was still with us. An entire year had passed since he insisted on returning to his apartment, a year in which he had indeed written new poems.

* * *

On New Year's Day, the phone rang. "Oh, hello, Katie," a nearly inaudible voice said when I answered. "It's Robert. I'm sorry to say I'm at the hospital. I had a little accident."

"Accident?" I echoed.

"Yes. I've broken my hip."

"When did this happen?"

"Last night. They did surgery this morning."

"What kind of surgery?"

"Hip replacement. I have a new hip."

With each new revelation, my sense of alarm grew, but Robert reported this latest news with a detached calm.

"Is it very painful?"

"It was last night. Excruciating. But it's not bad now. They have me on some drugs."

"It's quite impressive they could do the surgery so quickly."

"Yes, they didn't want to waste any time."

I thought of the fact of the holiday and gave a breath of thanks for all the people working New Year's Eve and New Year's Day who had made this latest miracle possible.

"How did this happen? Did you fall?" I asked.

"I'm afraid so. Rather clumsy of me."

I knew without being told that he must have tripped over the line to the oxygen machine that crisscrossed the floor of his apartment. I asked how long he would be in the hospital. A couple more days, he thought, and then he would go to Edgewood for rehab. The old routine. I was scheduled to leave for a meeting with freelance clients in Connecticut in the morning. I explained that I wouldn't be able to visit until I returned.

We were saying our good-byes when Robert interrupted me. "Oh, I wanted you to know. I sent the absentee ballot in last week. You'll be glad to know that's taken care of. I voted."

He voted, I later learned, for Kucinich.

I returned from my business trip and tracked him down at Edgewood by calling the nurses' station. Robert reported that they had him up and walking around already and were talking of sending him home in a day or two. I said how happy I was to hear this. There was one thing, though, he said. They had told him he had congestive heart disease. He delivered this information in a characteristically unemotional tone, one more fact about his body to be recorded but not lingered over. Would this signal a new stage in his illness? He gave no indication.

* * *

"I've left instructions that you are to be in charge of the contents of this place when the time comes," Robert said.

He made this announcement just as I was rising from my chair, about to leave his apartment a month later. As he had done earlier when he appointed me honorary next of kin in medical matters, he presented this as something that had already been decided and accomplished. My agreement was not necessary. I met his gaze and nodded.

Since returning home, Robert had been doing well. He was able to walk again with the walker, and his breathing seemed as good as it ever had. His recovery from the hip surgery was one more remarkable comeback.

My first thought, as I left his place and went out to my car, was of his poems. Were there unpublished poems in the folders stacked on the bottom shelf of the bookcase, treasures just waiting to be found? How eager I would be to go through those folders, if that in fact was what happened. I didn't know what he meant by "instructions" or who would find them. I should have asked him, but stupidly, I didn't. He had, as usual, taken me by surprise and then, also in typical fashion, closed the conversation as quickly as it had begun. Despite my resolution to be clear about my role after the confrontation at Edgewood, I was taken off guard and silently agreed to this new development. I was anxious at the thought of what it would mean to arrange for the disposal of his possessions, such as they were, but this seemed an inconsequential assignment compared to inheriting those folders of poems. The job of literary executor was one I would be honored to take on.

* * *

Robert managed to stay out of the hospital until May. This time the call came at two a.m. I slept right through the ringing phone, but Jim answered it. He didn't bother to wake me. "It was the medic alert people," he told me in the morning. "They called to tell you Robert went to the hospital."

"The medic alert people?" I could not think who he meant.

"The bracelet he wears. They said you're the contact person in an emergency."

"I had no idea."

"Robert didn't tell you?"

"No."

Since breaking his hip, Robert had worn the bracelet in case he fell again. I was certain he did not know when he put me down as the contact person that they would call me whenever the alarm went off.

It had become harder to find books for Robert, but since our house is bowed under the weight of books, with new volumes always being added to the collection, it was not impossible. I set off for the hospital that afternoon with some I thought he had not yet read in a canvas bag.

He was propped up in bed, a thin pillow wedged behind his back. His bare arms looked more skeletal than usual. "Ah, Katie," he said as I took a seat. I waited for more, but he simply gazed at me. Today the speaking of my name was enough.

"You discovered I was here," he finally observed.

"Yes. The medic alert people called."

"Who?" he said.

"Your bracelet. The alarm went off."

"Oh, I see. Yes, they called the ambulance for me."

His breathing was labored, his face wan and yellowed. I asked the usual round of medical questions. There was talk, he said, of sending him home in a day or two.

"I have made it clear I will not go on that ventilator again," he said. "If it comes to that, I say no. I've left instructions." His look was pointed. "And I don't want any nonsense about last rites. You understand?"

"Yes," I said.

"I won't have that."

I nodded, taken aback by his vehemence.

"Some chaplain came in to visit, and I sent him off. I don't need a chaplain."

Despite his feeble voice and rasping breath, he managed to sound militant. His hostility toward the church ran deeper than I knew.

This business dispensed with, Robert turned to lighter topics and a lighter mood, asking after my writing. I told him I was going to the Poetry Hoot that night.

"Ah, yes," he said. "I'm sorry to miss it. I don't think we ever believed it would be such a success when we started out. Quite amazing, isn't it?"

I smiled. "Quite." He had made the same statement, in almost the exact words, many times before, but I pretended I was hearing it for the first time.

When I said I should be going, he reached into a pile of papers on the bedside table. "I wondered if you could keep this for me."

He handed me a small piece of yellow paper on which he had written the lines of a poem.

"It's finished, or at least I think it is," he said. "I thought maybe you should hold on to it for safekeeping."

"May I read it?"

"Certainly."

The handwriting was a bit shaky, but clearly legible. The poem was not up to his usual presentation standards, as he was lacking the heavy linen paper he had at home and his fountain pen, but the words were sharp as ever.

Walking by day through the
Historic District you feel uneasy,
as though someone was trying to
tell you something, and that untrue.

But at night the whispers tell
how Flash Charley passed out right
in Pig Turd Alley, and what
Gimlet Alice said to the piano
player before she and everyone else
stopped being.

I looked up from the scrap of paper. Here was Robert in top form. "It's great," I said. "I love it."

He inclined his head. "You think so? I'm afraid my judgment may be clouded."

"No. It's terrific. The ending reminds me of Frank O'Hara, 'The Day Lady Died.' How does that go? The line at the end about how everyone stopped breathing."

His eyes brightened at this reference. "I guess it is similar."

"It has a similar cadence. I love that poem of O'Hara's."

"Yes, it's quite wonderful."

"But your ending is even more haunting. 'Everyone else stopped being.'"

"Hmmm." He said nothing more.

"I picked up O'Hara's *Lunch Poems* in a used bookstore somewhere years ago. I didn't even know who he was. I just liked the look of that little book. It's perfect. They are poems you could read over lunch."

"Those are the best poems, aren't they?" He raised his eyebrows for emphasis. Nothing made him happier than this sort of talk.

Our exchanges, like this one, went more easily in the hospital. Robert was more relaxed, freed of the burden of taking care of himself so diligently. Others did that for him here. He became his serene self again, and we fell into the rhythm of talk that was not pressured or anxious, that expanded to fill the time we had been given.

After a few more observations about Frank O'Hara, I rose to go. "Thank you," I said, waving the poem in the air.

He bowed his head. "No, thank you."

I left the hospital holding the scrap of yellow paper between my fingers like some bit of treasure dug up at an archaeological site. I placed the poem in my folder marked "Work by Robert Dunn" in the file cabinet in my office. Robert never mentioned it again, and the poem did not turn up among those he had Anne from the Poet Laureate board type up so he could give them to his visitors in the months that followed.

16.

Minor Poets Have More Fun

"The hospice people were here today," Robert told me when I called him at his apartment. He was home again, having avoided a stay at Edgewood this time.

"Hospice?" I echoed. This was the first mention of hospice since the disastrous meeting at Edgewood a year and a half earlier.

"They've been coming for a couple of weeks now." Robert offered this information with an easy nonchalance, as if it were already known to me.

"That's good," I observed somewhat lamely. "Are they helpful?"

"Oh yes, quite. The chaplain came to visit."

"And how was that?"

"She's not a bad sort, as chaplains go. Lutheran. I told her I wanted no nonsense about last rites. And no funeral. I've left instructions that there is to be no funeral."

I took this in without comment.

"We mostly talked about books," Robert added. "She was quite interested."

I liked this chaplain already; she had clearly read Robert correctly and understood that books were just another form of religion.

The arrival of the hospice caretakers did not seem to signal a substantial change in Robert's condition, simply another layer of services. The monitoring of his situation had been shifted from the nurse's aides over to them. They came in a few times a week, and on one of my visits I arrived just as they were leaving. The social worker was the same one who had attended the meeting at Edgewood; the nurse was someone I had not encountered before.

The social worker gestured toward the window. "Robert has something new."

I followed her gaze to a small air conditioner that fit neatly in the window frame. It made a low, not unpleasant, whirring sound. I did not look at Robert.

The women teased Robert in upbeat and cheerful tones as they said good-bye. I felt an overwhelming gratitude for their presence. Someone else understood. Someone else was responsible for providing the care I couldn't.

After the women had left, Robert fixed his gaze on me and said, "I'm glad I have the air conditioner. I wouldn't be alive without it."

* * *

Robert was seated in his new wheelchair, waiting for me and Jim in the lobby, with the oxygen canister perched in his lap. His chinos and short-sleeved shirt looked less rumpled than usual. I pushed him out to the street and over two blocks to RiverRun for the launch of Mimi's new book, *The Last Island*.

The rows of folding chairs inside the bookstore were occupied, and people lined the bookshelves along the walls. A moment's hush came over the room as I pushed Robert through the door. I stepped back to let a crowd surround him. This was the first time to my knowledge that he had made it to the bookstore since his reading in November, seven months earlier.

He nonchalantly greeted one person after another as though his attendance at this event were nothing out of the ordinary. He sat there holding court, clearly delighted to see so many old friends and to be the center of attention. The wheelchair suited him, I thought. He could talk without too much effort. He didn't have to approach people; they came to him.

Mimi gave a wonderful reading of her poems, and Robert waited with the others in line to have a copy of the book signed. In exchanges that were muted but emotional, one person after another sidled up to me and thanked me for bringing Robert. I knew that many of these people had assumed they would never see him again.

It was a perfect June day, bright and clear. We pushed Robert back to his apartment with a sense of triumph palpable among the three of us. He had lived to see this day, and we had made it to the bookstore and back. With each new step in the progress of his illness, we faced what had been unthinkable only days or weeks earlier. This time it was his need for a wheelchair. Such developments, like the oxygen lines threaded into his nose twenty-four hours a day, quickly became unremarkable, even routine. Robert adapted, without comment or complaint, and we went on. When I remember the afternoon of Mimi's reading, it's not Robert in a wheelchair I see, but Robert alive, flashing that conspiratorial smile, as if to say, "Didn't expect to see me here, did you?"

* * *

A month later, Jim went off to help friends cut wood one morning while I prepared to leave for my teaching residency. I had just about finished loading my luggage into the car when our friends called to tell me that Jim had fallen from a ladder as he was trimming a tree branch and was on his way to the hospital. In the emergency room, I found him on a gurney, a stoic expression on his face. His hip was broken, but a surgeon was on call and could do surgery that afternoon. Two pins were set in the bone to hold the hip together, and less than twenty-four hours later, a nurse loaded Jim into a wheelchair and brought him out to the parking lot for the ride home.

Because Jim was only fifty-one, the doctor elected to repair the hip rather than replace it. This meant that he would be on crutches, unable to put weight on the leg or drive, for three months, a longer and more challenging recovery than if he had undergone a hip replacement. The hope was that this would save the hip and forestall the need for a replacement, should it eventually become necessary.

I could not cancel my teaching residency and left Jim in the care of friends and his mother for ten days. The weeks after his accident come back as a confused and overwhelming blur, a series of unexpected decisions that had to be made, plans changed, logistics plotted. Everything revolved around the need to get Jim from one place to another, and the need to get him well. I felt, as I never had before, like a mother bear defending her cub, protective of Jim, constantly watchful, and frightened of how dramatically our lives had changed. The healing of the hip was not a foregone conclusion, and it would be a year before we would know if the surgery was successful. I struggled, without much success, to accept uncertainty as a condition of each day. Whether Jim would ever again spend the morning stacking a cord of wood and the afternoon riding his bicycle thirty miles, as he had earlier that summer, remained an unknown. While he lay on the couch, I moved through the house in an alternately numbed and frantic state as though searching for the man I used to know.

I wondered how Robert was doing, but I did not find the time to call him. A couple of weeks after the accident, an envelope arrived addressed to Jim in Robert's precise hand. A mutual friend of ours had stopped to talk with Robert when he found him sitting outside his apartment building one afternoon and told him about the accident. Robert expressed his condolences and said he knew how Jim was feeling, having gone through it himself, and hoped that he would be walking again soon.

I thought of Robert often as Jim hobbled around on crutches and passed long nights in pain. Robert's broken hip had been one more crisis for which I did not have time. As I helped Jim in and out of the car and brought plates of food to him, I wondered how Robert had managed without someone to do these things for him. How brave and stubborn he had been, and how little I had fully appreciated the depths of his determination.

* * *

I was away for much of July, and then away again in August. I knew that others, like Liz and Nancy and Anne, would be checking on Robert while I was gone, and he had the hospice nurses now. I left with the awareness that I might not see him again, although even with the arrival of hospice care, he seemed to be in another holding pattern, his condition no more critical than it had ever been.

I drove Jim to Vermont at the beginning of August for his teaching residency in a low-residency program at Goddard College. They set him up in an apartment that was handicapped accessible and drove him around campus in a golf cart. I left him with his colleagues and friends and went to our cabin an hour away. I had a week by myself at the cabin, time spent writing and reading and attempting to reestablish something of a work routine, before my sister and her family arrived to visit. It was

not until the final week of August, after Jim and I had some time together at the cabin, that we arrived back in Portsmouth. A message was waiting on the answering machine. "Oh, hello, Katie," Robert said, sounding
the way he often did, surprised to be speaking at all. "I'm in the hospital.
I thought I should let you know." I had to strain to catch the soft, garbled
words, and before I had quite gotten them, the message ended.

I went to the hospital the next day. He was propped up in the
bed by the window, a newspaper in his hands. The other bed was
empty; no roommate this time. From the window there was a view
of a rooftop, long and flat and topped with black gravel. Beyond the
roof, rows of brightly colored cars shone in the parking lot.

He looked up from the paper and said hello. The room was quiet, with no nurses present, no breathing machine running. "How was
Vermont?" he asked.

"Good," I said. "I just got back yesterday."

"I thought you must still be away." He folded the newspaper and
set it on the table by the bed. "Did you have any bears?"

"No, no bears this time. How long have you been here?"

"Three days."

"Have you had any visitors?"

"You're my first."

I was the one to alert people when Robert went into the hospital, but I had not been in town to do so. He did not seem unhappy
about the lack of visitors. I had the impression, as I had in the past,
that the time in the hospital was a relief, because here he was left
alone more than in his apartment.

Jim was still on crutches, and I was driving him to work and his
doctor's appointments. I was tired and irritable, anxious to return to our
old patterns, but that afternoon, I stepped into Robert's pool of quiet.

My questions answered, we sat in silence. I resisted the urge to
rush in and fill that silence. There was a stillness to Robert that day,

and an emptiness to the room and the hall outside, uncharacteristically quiet, that asked me to stop and be still, too. I felt my mind slowing down, as if it had been running for a long time and now, in this pause, was in danger of tripping over itself.

"Have you been reading anything?" I asked finally.

He pointed to a collection of poems on the table. I surmised that this trip to the hospital had been more planned than most. He had brought books with him.

He told me what he thought of the poetry collection. Our talk moved from this to poets and poems we loved, Shakespeare among them.

"Do you have a favorite Shakespeare play?" I asked.

"That's like choosing a favorite child, isn't it? But I guess I would have to say *Twelfth Night.*"

"I love that one, too. I wrote a paper on it in graduate school. I wanted to write about what Shakespeare does with gender in that play—Viola dressed as a man pretending to be a woman—but my professor said I was imposing a contemporary sensibility on Shakespeare. Shakespeare didn't write about sexual identity, he said."

"Nonsense," he said. "Of course Shakespeare wrote about sexual identity. What in the world is that play about if it's not about identity of all sorts, gender being one of them?"

"That's what I thought. The fact that men played women's parts back then does not explain everything he does in that play. He had to be conscious of it. I decided I would write the paper I wanted to write anyway. I went to the library and found something Harold Bloom wrote that backed me up. I figured if I brought in Harold Bloom, the professor would have to accept my argument."

"And what was that argument?"

"That Shakespeare presented sexual identity as something that wasn't fixed, that was fluid."

Robert nodded in agreement. "The scenes with Malvolio are quite wonderful. There's nothing like a good tragedy, of course, but I've always liked *Twelfth Night.*" He leaned forward, his face flush with happiness.

I took my leave a short time later believing I would see Robert again but knowing that if I did not, this would serve as good-bye, and it was enough. As I crossed the parking lot, I glanced up at the brick facade of the hospital in search of his window. I couldn't locate it. I didn't imagine he would be sitting there watching for me in any case. He would be absorbed in his reading again.

On that day, as we sank into talk about Shakespeare, and all awareness of Robert's condition and the sounds and smells of the hospital fell away, I glimpsed what it seemed Robert had been trying to show me all along: There was no script for dying, or living, for that matter. There was only what was before us, in all its messy confusion and imperfection, disappointment and fear, radiance and joy. He had shown me what it means to accept and embrace whatever life gives you. There had been times, naturally, when Robert was not that surrendered, when I had seen him fight what was happening to him and try to impose his will, just as I routinely did in response to the large and small stuff of my life. At this visit, he was serene again, centered fully in each moment, reminding me of what I would always love about him.

* * *

A few days later Robert called to tell me he had been moved to Edgewood. This time he was in a double room with a roommate. I found him dressed in an oversized yellow polo shirt and baggy chinos, seated in the chair by the bed. His roommate, a large man, sat on the other side of the room singing softly to himself. I saw that he held a Bible in his hands.

Robert raised his eyebrows when I met his gaze. He had the oxygen tubes threaded around his ears and going into his nose as usual, but he was not hooked up to the noisy machine for one of his treatments.

"Good afternoon," the man called out. He did not appear to be impaired. His eyes were clear, and he looked fit enough.

"Good afternoon," I replied.

"Hot out there?" he asked.

"Not too bad."

"We're comfortable in here, now, ain't we?" He grinned broadly and nodded toward Robert.

"Yes, we are," Robert said.

The man opened the Bible and began muttering to himself in a low undertone. I caught the word "lord" interspersed between others I could not make out.

Robert and I regarded each other in silence for a moment. The mumbled prayers would be a backdrop to our conversation, it appeared. "Did someone bring you clothes?" I finally asked.

"No, they turned these up somewhere here. They're a little big." He lifted the hem of the shirt that hung below his waist. "Better than nothing, though."

After trading bits of news, we turned to the upcoming Democratic Convention. Though Robert had voted for Kucinich in the primary, he had come around to sharing my enthusiasm for Obama.

"It's good to be going out on such a hopeful note," he said.

I had to think for a moment before I realized that in using the phrase "going out," he was referring to himself.

"I'm not sure we could have imagined this happening," he added. "We certainly hoped it would, but I don't know that we dared imagine it would happen this soon." I understood he meant the election of an African-American as president.

"The Civil Rights Act wasn't that long ago, at least in historical time," I said.

"No. Of course we have a long ways yet to go, but this is a step. It's a very hopeful note to go out on." He repeated the last phrase like a sort of mantra and added, "Oh, I almost forgot. I finished your book."

He took a manila folder stuffed with typed pages from the table and handed it to me. I had given him the second half of the book back in early July.

"It was quite interesting to see what you did with it," he said.

I waited for him to say more, but he simply sat there with that far-off expression on his face. I remained silent until I could stand it no longer. "You think it hangs together?" I said.

"Oh, yes."

"Do you think the different points of view work?"

"I should say so. I liked the way one informed the other."

We sat in silence for another long moment.

"I struggled with that," I said. "Making all the points of view work."

"I imagine that was quite a challenge. I thought you pulled it off admirably." After a moment, he added, "I did wonder about the veteran. I thought perhaps you could show the manuscript to a Vietnam vet who might know more about all that than I do."

"What was wrong with the veteran?"

He gave me a slightly alarmed look. It was difficult to get a reaction of any sort out of Robert, and nearly impossible to catch him off guard.

"Nothing," he said, perhaps too quickly. "I just thought someone who knows more about being in Vietnam might be good."

If Robert had been stronger, I might have pushed him to say more, but it was obvious that even this bit of conversation had exhausted him. I would have to be satisfied with the startled expression on his face, which told me, I thought, that I needed to do more work.

An aide entered the room. "Ready for your treatment?" she asked. Robert nodded. I took it as my cue to go. As I rose from the chair, Robert said, "I do have one favor to ask. I was wondering if you could go to my apartment and go through my books. I'd like to give them away. I was hoping I would get back there to do it myself, but I'm not sure that will happen. And the painting on the wall of the Athenaeum. Could you take that to Dick at the library? He's done so much. I'd like him to have it."

I nodded my assent to these tasks, though I couldn't think when I would find the time to execute them, and said good-bye. The folder with the pages of my book gripped in one hand, I made my way to the car.

Two days later, Robert called. "Have you gone through the books?" he asked.

"I haven't had time to go to your apartment yet," I said.

"I'd like to know this has been taken care of." His voice was impatient and insistent. "I don't think I have much time left." This pronouncement was of a new character, full of urgency.

"I have to take Jim to the doctor, and I have a few other things going on," I said. "Maybe I could go over on Wednesday or Thursday."

"Of course Jim should be your first priority." His tone was icy, laced with something that sounded almost like sarcasm.

In the pause while I tried to compose a response, the last three years were reduced to a simple equation. He had laid it out in stark terms—he might be dying, but he was not someone who took precedence. There was both accusation and disappointment in his words.

I felt in that moment I had not been the person Robert needed, though I saw with equal clarity that the person he needed did not exist, because he had not allowed this person to exist. He had spoken the truth this time. Jim was my first priority, and I was not going to deny it. Instead I made some vague promise about going to his apartment and hung up.

I found myself wishing that I could have made this time closer to what Robert desired, though I knew it was impossible. If he had truly wanted me there beside him, I might have been able to take on that role, but he didn't want me there beside him. He wanted me to make his solitude possible, to grant him somehow the ability to remain independent and in control, to preserve his silent hours. I couldn't give him that.

Robert had been on the verge of death so often. This crisis did not seem to be any different from the others. His condition did not appear to be any better or worse than it had been countless times before, and I was not sure how seriously to take his declaration that he did not have much time left.

* * *

The following day I drove Jim to his physical therapy appointment and in the parking lot met the hospice workers who had been caring for Robert. Their office was next to the physical therapist's, something I had not realized until that moment. I stopped them as they were getting into a car.

"How do you think Robert is doing?" I asked. "Have you seen him this week?"

"Yes, we've been to Edgewood," the nurse said.

"He seems to be holding his own," the social worker added. "We're a little worried that he's lost so much weight."

I smiled. "He hasn't lost weight. That's what he's always weighed. He's looked like that for twenty years. He's saying he doesn't think he has long to live. Do you think he's right?"

"Sometimes the patient knows when the end is near, and sometimes they don't," the nurse said. "It's not predictable."

"I haven't been able to visit him much this summer," I said.

"You've done so much. He really appreciates it. He's told us how much you've helped him. He finished your book last week. He was very happy about that."

I took these words in gratefully.

"He wants to die at home," the social worker said.

"Do you think that's possible?" I asked.

"We can't provide the level of care he needs right now," the nurse said. "If there's any way we can make it happen, we will, but it doesn't seem likely at this point. He's such a wonderful man. I can see why everyone loves him so."

The social worker nodded in agreement, then added, "He says he has no regrets, but I'm not sure that's true."

I thanked them for all they had done, aware that without them Robert would not have been able to stay in his apartment for the last four months. With that, we said good-bye and climbed into our cars. This conversation reassured me, both that I did not need to put too much stock in Robert's assertion about how much time he had left and that arrangements for getting him home, if this was possible, were in others' hands. But I drove off with the social worker's last comment echoing in my mind. What did she believe he regretted?

* * *

A small square of paper fluttered from between two books as I took them from the shelf. It was a faded tan color, and printed in the center, in a flowery script with a scrolled border, were the words "Minor Poets Have More Fun."

"Look," I said, holding it up for the others.

They paused in their sorting of the piles of books on the floor. "I remember that," Marie said. "Robert used to pass those out like calling cards."

Marie and Liz had agreed to meet me at Robert's apartment that afternoon to go through the books. After my conversation with the hospice workers, I was no more convinced now than I had been at any time in the past three years that Robert was near death, but I had managed to get to his place on Tuesday, earlier than I predicted.

I sat on the floor and gazed at the card in my hand. *Minor poets have more fun.* This is what Robert had been telling me since those first days when I watched him walking along Pleasant Street. There is no joy in the struggle for recognition, for money and fame and all they entail, but there is joy in the thing itself, the making of the poems. I saw now, through the lens of this startling little declaration, that Robert did not settle for being a minor poet, he *aspired* to be a minor poet. How incredible this was to me, one who aspired to be a major novelist and settled for being a minor one, with fun having little to do with it. Robert understood the gift of insignificance.

We had come up with a list of local writers who knew Robert and might like to have his books. We held up candidates as we pulled them from the shelves. "Who should have Jane Kenyon?" I asked. "I've already got this book."

"So does everyone else," Liz said.

We all paused and stared at the familiar cover; then Marie suggested someone who just might not own it. I marked the title on our list beside the person's name.

Robert's books filled four shelves of a long bookcase, and there were more perched in piles on top and on the floor. Most of the volumes were poetry, though he also owned a number of titles on Greek, Roman, Celtic, and medieval history; mythology; philosophy; nature study (including some very worn guides for identifying snakes and trees); and Native American culture. Thoreau, Plato, Swinburne, Chaucer, Kunitz—we set them in stacks. I placed some of the Native American books and ones on medieval and Celtic history aside for my teenaged nephew, who was interested in history and ancient cultures. I set the large number of Blake titles, most of them worn paperbacks with the covers falling off, in a box for myself. The collection of Greek and Roman history and poetry went into another box. I would take these to the Poetry Hoot for anyone who wanted them.

We finished sorting through the books in under an hour. As we gathered up the piles we had each agreed to distribute, I said, "Do you think I should take the folders of poems?"

A stack of manila folders remained on the bottom shelf of the bookcase. On the floor a couple of cardboard storage containers held more. Though he had told me he had left instructions that I was to inherit the contents of his apartment, I was not sure that these instructions would be followed.

"Yes," Marie said. "Take them. His family doesn't want them."

I scooped them up and added them to the box with the volumes of Blake.

That night I called Robert to let him know we had taken care of the books.

"Ah, thank you," he said. "That puts my mind at ease. I am sorry there is so much to go through in the apartment. I was hoping to take care of it myself."

"I took your papers, too," I said. "I have them at my house."

"Good. That's for the best."

"And I delivered the painting to Dick. He was very grateful."

"He's done so much."

Robert spoke clearly and strongly that night on the phone. Though he did not believe he would return to the apartment, I thought it was possible, just as it had turned out at so many unlikely junctures before, that he would.

* * *

Inside the nursing home, the air took on a neutral quality, neither warm nor cool. Outside the sun lay a thick layer of heat across the parking lot, but in the dark corridors, the controlled climate suggested an absence of summer or any other time of year. My skin felt suddenly dry, the life sucked out of it, as Hildy and I threaded past men and women perched in wheelchairs, many of them wrapped in blankets.

We found Robert seated by his bed, dressed in the same ill-fitting clothes. Hildy, a poet and teacher visiting from Sweden, where she had moved a few years earlier when her husband took a job there, knew Robert from the days when we served on the Poet Laureate Program board together. Robert lifted his head as we entered, clearly happy to see her.

Hildy took the remaining chair in the room and pulled it up beside the bed. She asked how he was doing in a tone that was upbeat, making the exchange feel natural, even easy. I went off to run a couple of errands. I knew it would tire him to talk with both of us. Let Hildy take my place today, I thought. The change would be welcome.

When I returned, their heads were drawn together, and Robert's expression was animated. They had been reciting poems by Ronsard, they told me, in French. This was something I was incapable of doing, and I was grateful to Hildy for her knowledge of languages and countless other things. She could easily match the reach of Robert's intelligence.

When Hildy rose from the chair, Robert handed me a card from the table by the bed. "I wondered if you could take care of this for me," he said.

I took the oversized postcard and saw, when I turned it in my hand, that it was a change of address form issued by the post office. In his familiar handwriting, there was the street and number of Robert's apartment under "old address." Beneath "new address," he had printed the number and street for the nursing home.

"I don't think I will be getting out of here," he said, and now his tone was short and clipped. "You better file that with the post office." I understood the significance of this gesture. He was giving up. I slipped the card in my back pocket, unable to think of any response, heavy with the sense that this had not gone the way either of us might have imagined or wanted. Once again, I felt that he was accusing me of not making possible the one thing he wanted, to die in his apartment alone.

Hildy and I said good-bye and made our way through the corridors to the main entrance. As we stepped into the hot, white light of midday, I asked myself, as I had many times before, why Robert had chosen me to be the family he did not have in Portsmouth. How did I come to be responsible for this untenable situation? How did this vigil, with its moments of such transcendence and grace, and moments of such conflict and pain, become my vigil, too?

The steps that led to this day can be retraced, even in some ways explained, but the larger question remained. Who was this brilliant, gentle man at whose side I had sat? One might imagine that by now I would have known him well, but in fact, in essential ways, I did not know him, not as I knew other friends. There was so much he kept hidden, so much he did not share. We were left gazing at each other across a silence he had cultivated and maintained determinedly. It was a silence that once seemed magical to me, at the core of what I most admired about Robert. How I envied his insistence that the world come to him on his terms. Now, in the harsh August sun, Robert's silence, and what it had asked of me, took on a different character, challenging my assumptions about not just his life but my own.

If I hadn't met Jim and taken the great leap into marriage, I might have followed a path more like Robert's. I could easily have gone on moving from place to place, making do with house-sitting gigs and sublets and frequently loading most of what I owned into a compact car. As I paint this picture now, it appears bleak, but there have been times when I longed for the freedom this other life seemed to hold. In the years when I knew Robert primarily as that intriguing figure passing on the street, he was a specter of the life I had left behind, the life I had not chosen.

Now, after the long journey of his illness, I could not romanticize Robert's solitude or my own. How much he needed people was abundantly clear and, by implication, how much I needed them, too. I seemed, just in the nick of time, to have snatched my home, my marriage, and my relationships with a world of family and friends from the jaws of my own foolishness. I might still feel most myself when seated at my desk, the silence of an empty house around me, but I could see now, as perhaps I could not before, that this had never been and never would be all that I, or my life, added up to.

* * *

Jim and I went to Vermont that weekend to harvest our end of summer vegetables. When we returned to Portsmouth on Sunday night, the routine of hauling bags full of zucchini and cabbage fell to me, as Jim was still on crutches. I saw the light on the answering machine flashing as I passed through the kitchen but ignored it. Jim hobbled out to the deck to start up the grill while I went about assembling a salad for dinner. As I set a bag of lettuce on the counter, I hit the play button on the answering machine. I had neglected to retrieve messages while we were away, something I usually did. The first message was a voice I didn't recognize. The woman identified herself as a nurse at the nursing home. She was trying to reach Katie Towler, she said. The second message was from the social worker. She thought I would want to know that Robert had passed away Saturday evening.

I went out to the deck and sank into a chair beside Jim. "Robert died," I told him in a voice drained of emotion, stunned that what had been inevitable for so long had finally happened.

Jim hugged me, and we sat there staring at each other without speaking, unable to believe or take in the news. Even an expected death is unexpected.

I tried to recall if Robert had seemed worse when Hildy and I went to see him. His breathing was labored, but no more labored than in the past. He did not look like he was dying that day, any more than he ever had. Would I have changed my plans for the weekend and stayed if I had believed him? This wasn't what he had seemed to expect or even want.

I struggled to find something good to hang on to, but our last visit kept coming back. I longed for an ending that might have been different, though I recognized that our final meeting was an extension of all that had come before, full of confusion, conflict, ambiguity, missed communication, and flashes of love.

I remembered the earlier visit at the hospital, when we talked about *Twelfth Night*. Our meeting at Edgewood, when Robert produced the change of address card, could not undo the clarity of that afternoon. Perhaps it was the days Robert had spent alone at the hospital that time, without informing anyone, that made him so powerfully present. He had recaptured a kernel of his solitude. The room was charged with the vitality of his mind, his passion for words used precisely and well, and the keen focus of a gaze that missed nothing. This is how I would choose to remember him, and how I would remember myself, perched on the edge of a vinyl-covered chair straining to catch each precious word.

From the notebooks of Robert Dunn

. . . .

Disconcerting how many of the people I love are dead or disreputable or both. Which makes the prospect of joining them quite acceptable. I told the woman from hospice that I would not like to outlive poetry by more than a single night. She seemed to find that a reasonable desire.

17.

East Rock

"I stayed all day Saturday," Robert's sister told me when I called her the next morning. "He couldn't talk, and he wasn't responsive, but I think he knew I was there. I sang hymns."

I hoped that Robert was not able to hear the hymns, or if he was, that they were a comfort somehow.

She was making arrangements for a funeral to be held at the church she attended in the town where they grew up. I said nothing about this, all too happy to let her take charge now. The service was for her, not him.

"Is it true that they're going to name a street after Bob?" she asked, her voice full of nervous excitement. "He just told me about this last week."

I explained I didn't know the details but that a proposal had been made to the city.

"Isn't that wonderful?" she said. "He was so pleased."

Clearly she was pleased, too, and impressed. I imagined Robert presenting her with this information in a final act of defiant pride. Now that he was gone, she could own his accomplishments.

"There's one thing I don't know about," she added. "He had a briefcase with him at the nursing home. I found instructions in it that he wants to be cremated and have his ashes scattered off the Isles of Shoals. I don't know what to do about this. Do you?"

These were unexpected instructions. I had never heard Robert talk about the islands ten miles off the New Hampshire coast, but I had been out to Star Island, a conference and retreat center, and said I would look into it.

* * *

A local historian called later that day. He was writing one of a series of articles about Robert that would appear in the *Portsmouth Herald* over the next week.

"There are a lot of characters in the history of Portsmouth," he said. "People who developed eccentric personas and became minor celebrities around town. Robert was one of these people, maybe the last of them. He was one in a long line of town characters, anyway, but the thing that made him different was that he was really good. His poetry was great. Most of the other town characters who wrote or made art were mediocre, but Robert could have had a national reputation."

Robert had led the life many of us wanted, he said, but didn't dare to imagine. "He was a professional reader, wasn't he? He saw to it that he could spend most of his time reading."

A professional reader. I liked the term. I saw Robert seated in the chair in his room on Whidden Street, the light tracking slowly across the wall as the day waned, a book in his hands.

The historian painted a portrait of Robert as someone who had craftily constructed a persona that allowed him to live as he liked and gave him an exalted status around town. "He created a myth about himself and then went about living it. It's really remarkable when you think about it. The less you know about a person, the easier it is to make a myth of them, right? Robert made sure no one knew anything about him."

Robert decided to be "a big fish in a small pond," he said. To be the Penny Poet of Portsmouth, that slight figure haunting the streets, was enough.

I had to agree with all of this, and yet there was a piece missing from this characterization of Robert. It was the piece, perhaps, that Robert himself had failed to take into account—the human element, and cost, of being the Penny Poet. Robert may have succeeded in making himself a blank slate on which others could trace their fantasies about the writer's life, but I could only think of the toll his austere existence had taken on him. For him, of course, it was a fair exchange for the poems.

* * *

When I arrived at the apartment, Robert's sister and her partner were already there, in the living room surrounded by cardboard boxes. Stepping into the small, dark room, I saw it through different eyes, my vision no longer tinged with the hope that Robert would make it back from the hospital or Edgewood. Without that hope, the place struck me as more bleak, his ragtag assortment of possessions shabbier and less substantial.

The hospice chaplain showed up shortly after I did, and we divided the tasks. Robert's sister took the kitchen, her partner the bedroom. I went through the living room, and the chaplain dealt with the piles of pill bottles on the folding table that had served as Robert's desk.

Robert had invested so little in owning anything that what he left behind felt devoid of emotional attachment. The contents of his apartment made a stark reminder, once again, of how sparely he had lived. To outsiders, these would have been the meager belongings of someone who was truly poor, but I knew just how rich Robert had been. He would be found now in his poems, not the things we sorted through.

Robert's sister held up a chipped yellow dessert plate with a border of flowers around the rim. "I think this belonged to our mother," she said before placing it in a cardboard box.

I recognized the plate, which my sister had purchased at the thrift store in Ann Arbor and I had given Robert, but I simply nodded. If believing it was their mother's brought some comfort, why tell her otherwise?

I sorted through the CDs and cassette tapes—Simon and Garfunkel, Édith Piaf, Gregorian chant. "Do you want any of these?" I asked.

His sister regarded the pile uncertainly. "No," she said finally. "Will you take them?"

I said I would and dumped them in another cardboard box. "What about this?" I pointed at a framed print on the wall of a bright patch of flowers in a garden.

"Did you give him that?" she asked.

"No."

"I don't know where that came from. I don't want it."

I added the print to the pile for the table in the basement where the residents of the building left anything to be given away. Robert's few pots and pans went in this pile, too, and a lamp with a torn shade.

Behind me the chaplain was crouched on the floor breaking open blister packs of pills and dumping them into a trash bag filled with kitty litter. This, she had assured us, was the way to dispose of the medications so they could be placed in the trash. She had been emptying bottles and blister packs for half an hour and still a good-sized pile remained in front of her. In the bedroom, Robert's sister's partner stripped the hangers of shirts and pants and loaded them into more trash bags.

There were a few books left that I had not gotten to the previous week. His sister said she didn't want them, even the small collection of literary magazines in which Robert's work had appeared. She didn't want the tea cozy in the shape of cat she had given him, either. She had bought one for herself, too. I slipped it in a box with the books. Among a few papers left on the shelves, I found a folder containing a photograph that appeared to have been taken in the 1930s or '40s of a man in a suit and a woman with long hair swept into a bun. I handed it to his sister.

"Our parents," she said, her eyes filling with tears. "My father was so handsome."

She reached for a tissue in her pocket and dabbed at her eyes, then returned to the tasks at hand. There was no time to linger on emotion, and moments later she was buoyant again, almost elated. I sensed, as I had the first time we talked after Robert's death, that she was filled with an uneasy happiness at being able to reclaim her brother at last. Two days had passed since then, and in that time, the tension of the past three years had been swept away. I could let her take her rightful place now.

I noticed a small, square magnet on the refrigerator door, with the words *Festina lente* stamped in bold letters across it and the name Aldus Manutius beneath them. I could not translate the Latin, but I slipped the magnet in my pocket. Later, when I examined it more closely, I found the translation in tiny letters on the magnet's back— "make haste slowly"—and the notation "Aldus Manutius: Venetian publisher, 1449–1515." A price sticker still affixed to the back read "Museum shop" with the price two pounds fifty. It must have been a gift from one of his traveling friends. The magnet remains on my refrigerator today, a fitting message from Robert.

The chaplain and I carried the collection of pots and pans to the basement and left them on the table outside the laundry room, above which a hand-lettered sign was taped to the wall with the single word FREE. By the time we made our second and third trips downstairs to the dumpsters out back with the bags of medications and other trash, most of what we had left on the table was already gone. I saved the print of the flowers and took it out to the lobby, where the toothless woman who always greeted me when I went in and out sat on the couch.

When I asked her if she would like the print, she beamed, pressed it to her chest, and rocked it like a baby. I heard her calling to someone coming through the front door as I made my way back down the hall. "Look what I got from Mr. Dunn!"

Robert's sister and her partner carried the furniture out to a truck—the chairs where Robert and I had sat drinking tea, the table and the bookshelf. The hospital bed, oxygen machine, and air conditioner had already been picked up by the agencies that had supplied them. I took the folding table Robert had purchased at the drugstore along with the toaster oven, both items his sister didn't want, though she was eager to have the microwave.

We had worked quickly and emptied the apartment in an hour and a half. I imagined someone going through my house full of stuff. It would take weeks.

* * *

The funeral was held a few days later up in Meredith. I had many excuses for not attending. Jim, still on crutches, needed rides to and from work and to his physical therapy appointment. The service was not what Robert wanted, and I was exhausted and overwhelmed.

I heard from others who attended the service that a couple of Robert's high school classmates were present and spoke when the time came for sharing memories. They recalled that Robert was rumored to have read every book in the town's public library and that while they were outside at recess, he was inside reading the dictionary.

The day after the service, a man arrived at my house with a shopping bag that held a cardboard box. He handed me the bag as he stepped through the front door. I peered at the box, inside of which were Robert's remains. It seemed far too small a container, and its delivery too strange and ordinary.

The man had attended the funeral and brought the container of Robert's ashes to Portsmouth at the request of his sister. He had known Robert through the Athenaeum and was a poet himself. He mentioned taking Robert out to dinner on occasion. I had never seen him before or heard his name.

"The executives of those cigarette companies should do jail time," he said before leaving. "They're the ones who killed Robert. We've lost too many people to COPD." He shook his head.

He was right, though I had never thought of assigning blame in that way. There was a certain irony, I saw, in Robert's addiction to a substance so representative of the rampant disregard for human life capitalism encourages, and his death from that addiction.

The shopping bag sat behind a chair in the living room for the next week, a reminder that this journey was not over yet. Robert's last request still needed to be fulfilled.

* * *

Liz passed out paper pirate hats while we stood on the dock waiting to board the boat for Star Island. One of the islands near Star, another in the string that make up the Isles of Shoals, was once supposedly a haunt of Bluebeard, and pirate lore is a part of the place. Robert would have approved of the hats. He had said to one of his visitors in the last months of his life, "If you do any sort of memorial, make sure you read funny poems." Liz had hit the right note.

The day was bright, hot, and still, a summer day in September. Nine of us took our seats on the narrow benches of the boat's deck— Liz, Marie, Ellie and her husband, and the hospice nurse and social worker. John and Mike, two local poets, joined us. No one from Robert's family came. His sister had left the arrangements entirely to me and made it clear she did not plan to be there.

The sound of the boat's engine drowned out the cries of the gulls circling overhead. Now that we were under way, this trip felt like something that was meant to be. The great space of water and sky was what I needed that day.

On the island, we skirted the knots of people on the long porch of the old hotel and made our way over the worn paths to East Rock. The manager of Star Island had given permission for the committal and told me that this was the spot where such services were usually held. We had arrived just before lunchtime, and the rocks were deserted, though the term "rocks" is misleading. They are more like cliffs, great rock faces that fall steeply down to the water. From other visits to the island, I knew that we were standing on the last bit of land between the United States and Portugal. Gazing over the expanse of water stretching before us under a cloudless sky, it seemed possible to see at least halfway to the next continent.

We sat in a circle on the rocks and shared memories of Robert and read his poems. People spoke as they were moved to speak, Quaker style. We laughed frequently. Many of the poems we had brought to read were indeed funny. The collective vision of Robert we created made him feel almost present, his eyes peering at us from behind his thick-rimmed glasses. We said no prayers. His words and the sea air were enough.

When everyone had spoken, I took the plastic bag of remains from the cardboard box and climbed with John down the rocks. The bag was held together with a twist tie, the way a sandwich bag might be. There was nothing sacred or ponderous in the gravelly pile of bone and ash. This is how Robert would have wanted it, too.

I removed the twist tie and, with John holding me by the arm, bent down to scatter the ashes in the direction of the water below us. The first handful blew straight back at me in the wind, leaving a fine residue on my pants. I was horrified, aware of those above us peering down over the cliff's edge. I am covered in Robert, I thought. This was clearly not how it was supposed to be done.

"This isn't going to work," I said quietly to John.

"We'll have to just toss the whole bag down to the water, not empty it," he said.

"No, we can't do that." Robert's last act could not involve littering. He would not want to add more plastic to the ocean.

John and I stared at each other, both of us clearly rifling through options in our minds, though we said nothing.

"I'll go down," John said finally. "I'll climb farther down."

We had gone, I thought, as far as we could go. The rock was almost a vertical face from here to the water, but somehow he managed to inch his way closer. He made it to a small perch, turned the bag upside down, and let the ashes fall. In seconds I could see them, spread in a growing circle of white in the water, a startlingly beautiful cloud that moved as the water moved in bands of light and dark. John took me by the hand, and we climbed back up the rocks to watch with the others as Robert went out into that great ocean.

On the way back on the boat, Ellie said that at first she thought it made no sense to have Robert's committal all the way out at the Isles of Shoals, but now she felt it was quite appropriate.

"Those were his instructions," I said.

"His instructions? I thought it was your idea."

"No," I said. "I wouldn't have come up with this." We both laughed.

"I almost called you and said we should leave his ashes in the river, in town," she said.

"I agree. That's where he belongs, in town. But this is what he wanted."

Liz joined us, and we asked her if she thought Robert had ever been to Star Island. She had no idea. Neither did anyone else in the group. None of us had ever heard him mention going out to the Isles of Shoals.

Robert's last difficult request, as I came to think of it while I made repeated phone calls and sent around strings of emails, struck me as another piece of myth-making. Why Star Island? It was too grand a gesture. But now I was abundantly grateful to him for bringing us together for this trip across the water. That wild and desolate piece of ocean did seem to be where he belonged. His last resting place is close to people but looking toward the infinite, and this is how he lived his life, amidst the community of Portsmouth yet fixed on a far horizon.

You have to live twenty years in a place to claim
never to have been there. Before that you're not quite sure.
There are everywheres everywhere.
A moment of shared laughter, a scent of new-cut grass
will give strangeness a familiar face.
Yet if my heart has a true home
it lies in ruins where people are foolishly
building anew. Where even now in the rubble
someone is clearing a path, and a sheet of transparent
plastic catches the wind like a guiltless flag.

—*Robert Dunn*

18.

In the Archives

We gathered at a restaurant on a street by the river for a reading in Robert's memory the April following his death. The downstairs bar was packed, every seat taken. Writers had driven across the state to be there.

A group of us had been asked to read, and one by one we made our way through the maze of tables to the microphone. Some read poems of Robert's; others read poems they had written in tribute to him. I went last and read two of the poems he wrote in the final year of his life. Afterward the floor was open for anyone to speak. A great bear of a man in his thirties came forward. I recognized him from the open mic at the Poetry Hoot. Over six feet tall with massive linebacker shoulders, he had always struck me as out of place among the collection of nervous poets who make their way gingerly to the microphone.

"I only met Robert a couple of times," he said. "One of them was here, two years ago, at the Jazzmouth reading. I bought a copy of his book and asked him to sign it. He wrote something in Latin. I still don't know what it says. After Robert died, I went to the Poetry Hoot, and there was a box of his books anyone could take. I took a collection of poems by Horace. I'd never read Horace before. It was kind of a surprise, but I've really gotten to like him. But every time I open the book, the smell of cigarettes nearly knocks me out."

He acknowledged our laughter and returned to his seat.

This was our memorial service, and it seemed to be what Robert would have wanted. People of all ages crammed together in the dark space of the bar, poems clutched in their hands and expectation on their faces—this was the sort of gathering where he was most comfortable.

* * *

The following winter, I went to the Poetry Hoot on a rainy night in early December. I hadn't attended the Hoot since just after Robert's death, and this night the booths along the wall and tables at the back were empty. Usually if I arrive fifteen minutes before the start of the reading, I have to stand, pressed beside others, near the coffee counter. It was the rain, I told myself, the wind gusting across the parking lot a few weeks before Christmas, but the absence of people mirrored other absences.

I took a seat by myself at a booth by the large plate glass window and stared out at the wet pavement in the parking lot as the first featured poet read. His voice, resonant and measured, told us he had a sure grip on where each poem was headed. Some he recited from memory, and they were complex poems, full of language that did not come simply or quickly, making his ability to learn them by heart that much more impressive. I felt like I was in church. It was not just the religious references in the poems and the beautiful cadences that mimicked the psalms. The silence surrounding his voice delivering the poems had a church-like quality, and with the chilly sweep of the parking lot beyond the window, I was able to lose myself in the pleasure of the words as if participating in some liturgical ritual. The mood was more church-like than church itself, and I found myself wishing that church were closer to this, with fuller spaces of quiet.

In the final years of his life, when he was still able to get to the Poetry Hoot, Robert would sit in one of the booths by the window. I was not seated in "his" booth, the one closest to the microphone. I was in the one farthest back, but when I raised my eyes to look at the poet, I saw Robert there in his booth, head cocked in a way that signaled his amusement with the scene. I thought of how we would talk about the readings afterward. He would make sly comments about some of the more exhibitionist characters who inevitably showed up for the open mic portion of the evening, but his remarks remained gentle, even kind, barely flirting with the catty or critical. He loved the bad poets as much as or more than he loved the good ones.

That night I was struck dumb by the depths of missing Robert. I had been busy, very busy, in the last year. This was why I hadn't made it to the Hoot, I had told myself, but I saw now that I was not ready to face the flickering image of Robert moving through the crowd. Suddenly I was missing not the idea of him or a memory preserved like a flower pressed between wax paper but Robert himself, his physical presence. Enough time had passed that I could reclaim the simple goodness of knowing him, and with this came the crippling realization, as though it had just happened, that he was gone. As I glanced around the room at the audience of poets with their faces turned toward the man at the microphone, I expected to catch Robert's eye, to see him give me one of those looks full of knowing mirth, as if he were saying, *what good fortune we have to be here, don't you think, on this absurd earth among these foolish and wonderful people.*

* * *

In the years after Robert's death, I went searching for him. I did not imagine when he was living that I would write a book about him, but so much between us still felt unsettled. Mystery remained at the core of my memories and our friendship. I began writing about Robert as a way to get to the bottom of those mysteries and quickly discovered that I was plumbing my own depths as much as his. The search for Robert became a search for myself.

I did not find much in the folders I took from Robert's apartment. There were no drafts and only a couple of poems I had not seen before. In the notebooks, there were only a few entries, most of which I have included here. He did not keep a journal, or at least did not leave one behind. He did not even keep copies of the penny books he published or of the literary magazines where his work appeared.

* * *

A photograph of Pig Turd Alley surfaced recently as part of a project to document the history of the old Puddle Dock neighborhood. It is not much more than a walkway between two houses, and there are no signs of pigs or their turds, but there it is, an actual place. I thought Robert had invented this unlikely name and put it in the poem he gave me that day in the hospital a few months before his death.

In his papers I can find only one poem written after this one, a short tribute to Joe Frost, the cousin of Robert Frost who worked in the used bookstore. Joe Frost died in July, two months after Robert gave me the historic district poem, and a month before Robert's own death. The piece he wrote in memory of Joe is typical of the occasional poems Robert sometimes sent to people with his letters. Fittingly, his last longer poem, the one about the historic district and Pig Turd Alley, is an elegy for Portsmouth and, by implication, an elegy for Robert himself. He was part of that world, peopled by the likes of Flash Charley and Gimlet Alice and the pigeon lady, that is gone now.

Robert's life was always unlikely, even in the rougher era when he came to town. Today his life seems far more than unlikely. The possibility he held out of living so completely outside the norm is that much harder to find in a place like Portsmouth now.

The latest round of development has brought a building boom to downtown. The small complex where the A&P was once located has been torn down, and on this site and surrounding empty lots, three hotels have gone up. When you drive into the city from the north end, you meet a wall of new construction that blocks the views of downtown and could be anywhere U.S.A. Other large-scale retail and condominium projects are in the works for this corridor and along the waterfront. What is happening in Portsmouth is no different from what is happening in thriving urban centers on either coast of America: the widening gap between rich and poor and the homogenization of our public spaces, with money, not a shared vision of community life, as the driving force behind it all. In a capitalist culture, progress is synonymous with profit. This is as true in Portsmouth as it is elsewhere, but my heart sinks when I see that wall of hotels, and I still long to spend the afternoon wandering the aisles of J.J. Newberry's in search of odd treasures.

Connie remained alone in her house on Whidden Street until she was in her mid-nineties, after Ed had been moved to an assisted living facility as the result of a broken hip. In 2013, Connie fell one night and was found by neighbors in the morning. She died two weeks later, and the house was sold. New owners gutted and rebuilt the place, and took down the apple trees in the backyard. For a year I watched the construction crew replace the roof, build a new front porch, install windows, and slap on paint, able to follow it all from my kitchen window. When the renovation was complete, the buyer put the house back on the market and quickly sold it. Connie's place looks like any other upscale house in the South End now.

* * *

I stepped from the car in the parking lot of the supermarket one afternoon recently and stopped to take in the clouds rimmed in a purple that approached black. The centers of the clouds were tinged in rose, suffused with an otherworldly light. I had driven through town without even noticing this fantastic display of color and light. Now I stood beside the car, keys between my fingers, the shopping list in my head and chores at home forgotten.

Sunlight and wind take me by surprise more often these days. Are the days more beautiful than they used to be, or am I simply more observant and attuned to my surroundings? The absolute goodness of this physical world in all its splendor is evident to me in ways it seems not to have been before. I am here more than I used to be, present in the day to day. The anxious anticipations, the strivings and imaginings, the worry about a host of things out of my control slowly fall away, bit by bit, and it feels as if I have woken up and discovered another life that was waiting for me all along.

The knowledge that one's days on this earth are limited, which didn't truly register until I was past fifty, gives a terrific sweetness and clarity to life. What once seemed to matter so desperately (how many copies one of my novels sold) is put into radical perspective. I want to notice the sky and have time and emotional space for people. I want to savor all that is precious about this life before it is gone. At the age I have reached, to experience joy when and if we can strikes me as our truest purpose. How thoroughly we thwart the possibility of joy, how we make our days about everything but joy. Robert's daily routine was rooted in a quiet joy. The walk into town. The words in his mind. The antique streets and antique houses. The people he met on the sidewalk, and the laughter he shared with them. I was caught up in the last years of his life in my frantic struggle to finish my novel and make my mark on the literary world. It's only now that Robert is gone that the lessons he had to teach fully reach me, fully hit home.

As I come closer to embracing the life I have been given, I move farther from the concerns that have ruled me for most of my years as a writer. The terrible weight of feeling I had to prove myself, and fearing that I would never measure up. The walling off of that part of myself that was necessary to do the work of the writing (only by guarding the privacy and silence fiercely could I maintain the little walled garden where the words would, if not flourish, at least poke their heads up). The constant inner attention to the characters and stories developing, shifting, growing, solidifying. How much concentration it took to be so watchful for anything I could put on paper.

Robert's secret was that he wrote for the pure pleasure of it, as a sort of Zen exercise, with no thought of where the poems would end up or how they would be received. He did not particularly care if they were ever read by anyone at all. Their purpose was in giving a shape to his days, offering a path for his mind to walk. They were, first and foremost, a form of play. He never lost sight of this.

His happiness, and I do believe he was happy on the most profound of levels, came from his ability to stay focused on what feeds the deepest center of the self. Although he maintained a moat of silence around his days in which the words could surface, he was very much in this world, present and attentive. He did not miss the changes in the sky or much else. I am vowing that I won't now, either.

Henry David Thoreau defined success with these words: "If the day and the night are such that you greet them with joy, and life emits a fragrance like flowers and sweet-scented herbs, more elastic, more starry, more immortal—that is your success." I copied this passage in my journal when I first read *Walden* in college, recognizing that it was wisdom I should live by, though I knew I could not put it into practice. Robert showed me what it would look like to take these words fully to heart. Through him, I saw that the hunger for recognition and success as it is defined in contemporary America is a hollow hunger, seldom satisfied. What I have truly hungered for is a harmony between my self and my writing and the living of a daily life. Robert achieved this harmony as no one else I have known.

* * *

I still look for him every time I walk into town. It does not seem possible that these streets, which defined Robert and were defined by him, can go on existing without him. I see him seated on the wall by the cemetery as I drive past, and slouching through Market Square. There is some comfort in these fleeting glimpses. I no longer have to remember Robert in his apartment or wheelchair. Death has restored him to the brick walkways where he is meant to be, where I knew him least but perhaps best.

On a recent night as I walked home from an event at RiverRun Bookstore in honor of Banned Books Week, Robert was there with me, as he so often is. It was the sort of event he would have gladly attended, and I imagined us talking about the readings of work by Galileo, Mark Twain, J.D. Salinger, Grace Metalious, and Walt Whitman. I imagined other conversations, too, ones that never would have occurred between us, but I wanted to tell him that I have grown a bit older and more forgiving of myself and others, a bit more patient with the unpredictable path of writing and life. I wanted to tell him that sometimes, for a moment or two, I walk the streets of Portsmouth now the way he did, full of gratitude and poetry.

I learned from Robert's ability to give up so much, though this wasn't how he saw it. I learned from his single-minded devotion to the writing. But I couldn't live that life myself. My way is made of greater contradictions and ambiguities. You could argue it's a richer and fuller life, but that is only true from a certain perspective. Robert's life was equally rich and full in its own way.

In *The Notebooks of Malte Laurids Brigge*, Rilke writes: "My God, if any of it could be shared! But would it *be* then, would it *be*? No, it *is* only at the price of solitude." For many years I believed these words, that only by going off on my own could I find what I needed for the writing. They strike me as less true now, especially after the time I spent with Robert. Writing, he understood, is a form of love, not just for the written word and the power of the imagination but for the world beyond the room where you write. Our work as writers is that "letter to the world," in Emily Dickinson's words, composed out of an intense desire to see our experience whole. Robert knew that this act of love that separates us from the daily commerce of living immerses us in it at the same time.

When I embarked on this book, I imagined that something would be waiting for me at the end. An answer? Some resolution? But what is waiting is just what was there all along, as Robert knew all too well: living from one day to the next, telling the stories that need to be told, taking a late-afternoon walk in town. "We're just going out," I hear him say as I step out the door. "Do you want anything from the ocean?"

Appendix

In the years since Robert's death, I have sought out people who knew him and tried to piece together a fuller biography for him. Those I have spoken with have added small pieces of the puzzle, but no one seems to know much. He remains a blank canvas on which people project their wishes for him, which turn out to be, more often, wishes for themselves. A few believe that Robert was gay, and this is the key to his carefully guarded privacy. Some of them tell me they saw him around town with a man they assumed to be a boyfriend in the 1980s. Someone else tells me she saw him walking around downtown holding hands with a woman for a brief period in the early '90s. I can't confirm the existence of either a boyfriend or girlfriend. Like much of what I have uncovered about Robert, these stories seem to fulfill a need to explain him in a way that proved elusive when he was alive, but perhaps the former Keeper of the Athenaeum, who hired him in 1987, put it best when she said, "He was rather unknowable."

At its core the effort to explain Robert assumes that something went wrong to make him who he was, but what if we, not Robert, are the broken ones dragging our money and possessions and ambition behind us? In our current age, every life story can be reduced to a psychological profile of wounds and their effects. Every quirk comes with a diagnosis, but Robert was not bipolar or depressed, and placing him in the category of heterosexual or homosexual seems beside the point.

In retrospect it feels inconceivable that Robert lived among us as he did, and abundantly clear how little we really knew about him. Here are some of the things I have learned about him since his death:

He bought the trench coat he always wore at the Salvation Army for ten cents.

Before getting his job at the Athenaeum, he worked at Wesley Varney, a salad factory in downtown Portsmouth that supplied condiments and macaroni salad to restaurants (hence the line he used in his bio about being a "poet enjoying his salad days"). He also worked as a substitute dishwasher at the Library Restaurant in the late 1980s.

He never got his driver's license. The driver's ed teacher at Meredith High School quit after having Robert in his class. He said it was impossible to teach him to drive.

The administration at Meredith High School decided Robert was too fragile to take physical education and allowed him to take an extra academic class instead. He may be the only person ever to have graduated from the school without fulfilling the requirement.

He was an early activist, joining a protest in 1961 at the University of New Hampshire, a refusal to take shelter in the event of a civil defense alert. He went on to protest the Vietnam war and, in the 1980s, was involved with the Clamshell Alliance and protests against the Seabrook Nuclear Power Plant in New Hampshire.

He went south in the summer of 1965 with the civil rights movement with a small group of Episcopalians from New Hampshire. Jonathan Daniels, who was shot and killed as he protected a young African-American woman attempting to enter a store in Hayneville, Alabama, had gone down ahead of the group. Robert would not talk about this experience, though others and I asked him about it directly. He did say once that he had known Daniels.

He was able to read French, German, Latin, and Greek, though he never studied any of these languages, except perhaps briefly, in school. In the notebooks left in his apartment, I found columns of English words with their translations into Native American dialects, including Penobscot, Micmac, Abenaki, and Algonquin. A couple of Xeroxed articles on Native American languages turned up in one of the folders. He never mentioned this project.

Starting in 1972, he picked apples each fall with the Greenleaf Harvesters, a group of peace activists who turned to apple picking because farm workers did not have to pay taxes on their earnings. In this way, they avoided supporting the Vietnam war. The group lived communally and specialized in picking for small orchards still growing heirloom varieties. Robert continued picking apples through the early 1980s and was secretary for the group, which tithed 10 percent of its combined earnings to such causes as the Vietnamese Buddhist Church and the Presiding Bishop's Fund for World Relief of the Episcopal Church.

Robert considered joining a monastic order in the Episcopal Church after graduating from college and later decided to become an Episcopal priest, but the admissions committee at Episcopal Divinity School in Cambridge, Massachusetts, said that he was not dynamic enough for the priesthood, and he gave up the idea. This is the most surprising piece of his biography that he did not reveal to me, although the fact that Robert, one of the more Christ-like people I have known, was not accepted into the church is no surprise at all.

* * *

Robert was profiled in various local newspapers over the years. Some of these articles were found in a folder among his papers marked "Vanity." Here is a collection of quotes taken from those articles:

On being a poet: "When I'm really doing my job as poet, I'm not speaking to you. I'm speaking for you." (*The Boston Globe*, January 18, 1988. Article by Clare Kittredge.)

On the kind of poems he writes: "Using a poem to drive home a point is a bit like using a violin for a hammer. It wouldn't make a good hammer, but afterwards it wouldn't be a good violin, either. That's why I avoid didactic poetry." (*The Wire*, August 30, 2006. Article by Courtney Denison.)

"I think basically a poem ought to say what it's got to say and get off the stage." (*Foster's Daily Democrat*, October 26, 1983. Article by James E. Bressor.)

On his beginnings: "I caught the bug (poetry)—let's see, I was about fifteen. I fell in love with the writer Shelley. I haven't dared look at him since. You don't want to profane a first love." (*The Wire*, August 30, 2006. Article by Courtney Denison.)

On his education: "I didn't start getting an education until I got out of school." (*The Boston Globe*, April 18, 1999. Article by Clare Kittredge.)

On the writing process: "I put marks on paper every day, but they generally wind up in the wastebasket. A wastebasket is a great resource for a writer, I think." (*The Wire*, August 30, 2006. Article by Courtney Denison.)

On copyright: "It just feels kind of silly posting no trespassing signs on my poems." (*The Boston Globe*, April 18, 1999. Article by Clare Kittredge.)

On making a living as a poet: "What I make would be a comfortable middle class income in any of the African countries. It seems graceless to complain. It's a topic that arises whenever two or three artists get together, a familiar rap. I've known painters and filmmakers who couldn't work because they didn't have enough money to buy materials. With me it's never been a problem. There's always a scrap of paper." (*Portsmouth Herald*, November 13, 1983. Article by Melanie Reisinger.)

On the similarity between apple picking and poetry: "It's something you do very gently with all your might." (*Foster's Daily Democrat*, October 26, 1983. Article by James E. Bressor.)

On people: "We're alike. I think human beings are more alike than unlike." (*Portsmouth Herald*, November 13, 1983. Article by Melanie Reisinger.)

On Portsmouth: "Walking through downtown Portsmouth, you get the feeling it's always been this way, even though it changes constantly." (*The Wire*, August 30, 2006. Article by Courtney Denison.)

On living in a small town: "You know who your enemies are." (*Foster's Daily Democrat*, October 26, 1983. Article by James E. Bressor.)

On war: "It's stupid, it's inconvenient, and we do it." (*Portsmouth Herald*, November 13, 1983. Article by Melanie Reisinger.)

On the civil rights movement: "We had our hearts thoroughly broken." (*The Boston Globe*, April 18, 1999. Article by Clare Kittredge.)

On the course of his life: "Everybody has one worse thing that can happen to them. If worse came to worse, I'd be teaching English at a small Catholic girls' school in the Midwest." (*Portsmouth Herald*, November 13, 1983. Article by Melanie Reisinger.)

On his knowledge: "I don't know a thing about baseball." (*Portsmouth Herald*, November 13, 1983. Article by Melanie Reisinger.)

On his living situation: "I'm always aware there are people without even one room." (*Foster's Daily Democrat*, October 26, 1983. Article by James E. Bressor.)

On being termed a "hermit," which he denied: "Any of us writers, we desperately need a few hours of quiet." (*Foster's Daily Democrat*, October 26, 1983. Article by James E. Bressor.)

Acknowledgements

M any people shared their memories of Robert Dunn with me as I was writing this book. I want to acknowledge in particular Richard Winslow, Clare Kittredge, Roger Cole, Lynne Crocker, David Diamond, the late Nancy Hill, Paula Rais, Marie Harris, Elizabeth Knies, Peter E. Randall, Franz Eslinger, Jane Porter, Ellie Sanderson, Gordon Carlisle, Dudley Laufman, Ronan Donohue, Dorothy Brown, Anne Dewees, and Pat Parnell. For invaluable feedback and encouragement, I am grateful to Ilya Kaminsky, Merle Drown, Peggy Hodges, Claudia Putnam, Robert J. Begiebing, Kelly Harrison, Andrew Periale, Mimi White, Hildred Crill, Anne Welch, and Carrie Sherman. For assistance with research, I am indebted to Michael J. Huxtable and Nicole L. Cloutier at the Portsmouth Public Library, Tom Hardiman and Carolyn Marvin at the Portsmouth Athenaeum, and Steve Fowle, Harold Whitehouse, Nancy Grace Horton, and Dennis Robinson. To my superb editor, Dan Smetanka, and the team at Counterpoint: You are every writer's dream. Thank you for seeing to the heart of this book and bringing it into the world with such expert care. I owe enormous thanks as well to my agent, Deborah Schneider, who has always championed my work and whose friendship has sustained me. To my husband, Jim Sparrell, I am grateful every day for the love, patience, and support that make our life together, and my life as a writer, possible.